TREES ACCORDING TO GOD'S PLAN

TREES ACCORDING TO GOD'S PLAN

Renee Bennett

Copyright © 2021 by Renee Bennett

All rights reserved. No part of this publication may be reproduced, distributed, or transmitted in any form or by any means, including photocopying, recording, or other electronic or mechanical methods without the prior written permission of the publisher. For permission requests, solicit the publisher via the address below through mail or email with the subject line "Attention: Publication Permission".

This publication contains the opinions and ideas of its author. It is intended to provide helpful and informative material on the subjects addressed in the publication. The author and publisher specifically disclaim all responsibility for any liability, loss, or risk, personal or otherwise, which is incurred as a consequence, directly or indirectly, of the use and application of any of the contents of this book.

ISBN	Paperback	978-1-956135-34-3
	eBook	978-1-956135-33-6

CONTENTS

Introduction 1
Reviews 7
Acknowledgement 9

Genesis 11
Exodus 16
Leviticus 18
Numbers 20
Deuteronomy 21
Joshua 24
Judges 25
1 Samuel 27
2 Samuel 28
1 Kings 29
2 Kings 33
1 Chronicles 35
2 Chronicles 36
Ezra 38
Nehemiah 39
Esther 41
Job 42
Psalm 43
Proverbs 46
Ecclesiastes 47
Song of Songs 48
Isaiah 50
Jeremiah 56
Ezekiel 60
Daniel 69
Hosea 71
Joel 73

Amos	75
Zechariah	76
Matthew	78
Mark	80
Luke	81
John	84
Acts	86
Romans	88
James	89
1 Peter	90
Jude	91
Revelation	92
Summary	95

REFLECTIONS

The Azalea and the Snail	99
Intention	101
The Disciple Whom Jesus Loved	102
Undulations Of Life	104
How God sees you…	106
Jeremiah 29: 11-14	107
Through one man…	109
Sun Swept	110
Turn, Turn, Turn	112
en(courage)	113
me versus You	114
Resonates	116
Singular	117
The Son Shine Effect	119
Puzzles	120
Sinister	122
Quiet the noise of the enemy!!!	125
Love on the Battlefield	127

About The Author	131

INTRODUCTION

I am just an ordinary girl, nothing fancy, not even a great childhood. God is an expert at taking the ordinary and doing something extraordinary with it. He has written my journey with Him in such a way that I just stand back in awe of it. I have journeyed around the world on missions, from my little hometown in Georgia. My heart has grown to love all kinds of people, as family. This book is not authored by a Bible scholar. It is simply an ordinary girl who loves God and loves to dig in His Word with His guidance and find amazing treasures, yet uncovered. My desire is that it sparks an interest in even just one more person catching that excitement for God and His Word.

Stepping out to lead ministry of any kind can be difficult and a little scary. Part of my journey has been an internal struggle with God, along the same lines as Moses when he was called to lead the Israelites. As the second year of leading Titus 2 Women's Ministry approached, I was getting more and more stressed out and somewhat desperate in my prayers to God. God are you sure I am the right person to do this? I've got issues, I am not perfect or even good enough. Isn't there someone who could do it better, who is more qualified? I sensed that the answer was, you are the one. So, with my protest noted, I said, "Yes". As our pastor, Darey Kittle often says, "God does not always call the qualified, but often the available." I then committed to be obedient and prayed, "What next Lord, what direction should we take this year as a group and what do You want me to do?" My answer was a little bit of focus and correction within my own walk. I felt the answer was, "What about finishing what I gave you last year? Trees."

The fall of the previous year, had its own struggles. I was doing Beth Moore's "The Quest" Bible study in our Weekday Women's study group and I came to the end of myself in week one. I was reading and it asked about questions I had for God. I thought there is no way I have questions for God. I am sure and certain in my faith. I am a leader in Women's Ministry, I teach the Bible to children here and around the world on missions (A bit of pride there). Yet, when the time came to write down questions for God, they just came flooding out of me. I was shocked and completely taken aback, to the point of questioning myself, my walk, my faith, my leadership ability. I was so deflated, that it depressed me. I spent a week questioning not only God, but myself as well. When I regained some composure, I picked the book back up and started to study again. I came to the statement, "Feeling that you have mastery of God is an indication that you have a lack of intimacy with God" (The Quest, Beth Moore). Well, there was my predicament. I was holding God at arm's length and displaying a lack of full trust in Him. I had fallen into the trap of trying to do it all in my own power.

I decided that I needed to go on a spiritual retreat until I found intimacy with God that I was lacking. However long it took, whatever I needed to do or stop doing, until I reached God in two-way communication AGAIN!

I went for a walk at a park in the woods and prayed for a word from God. It was early in the morning and no one was on the trail except for me, and God. I was walking along my second 2-mile lap and becoming weary and discouraged that I had not yet gotten a word from God. I was so focused in prayer that I wasn't paying much attention to my surroundings. I heard a rustling in the woods right beside me and jumped and ran. Then I heard a gobbling sound and realized it was wild turkeys in the woods.

I kept walking on mile 3 of this trek and begging God for a word. I asked God, "Do you want me to keep walking or to sit on the next bench and wait to hear from You? I sensed that I should sit and pray with eyes closed and listen for God. I felt a cool, gentle breeze. I waited and waited and waited. Then, I heard another rustling and gobbling sound and my eyes flew open. Then, I the word trees came to mind. Sounds like a strange word and it was not what I expected, but these are the thoughts that flooded my mind immediately:

Do you see the trees all around you? Can you count them? What if each tree represents a soul? Recall that you are to be as trees planted by rivers of living water. Recall when I restored sight to one blind man and the first thing that he saw was people walking around as trees. Recall the vision of the prophet seeing people walking around as living trees and dead trees. Notice the trees, the variety and shape and size.

- The tiny trees growing under the protection of the larger ones, until they are strong enough to stand on their own. Very much like children growing under the protection of their parents.
- The larger ones that start with beautiful smooth bark and then the bark becomes cracked and crusty as they grow older. So similar to the aging process that people go through.
- The trees that are damaged by natural forces or something man has done, such as cut away a branch. Every person that I know has been hurt or damaged by another person at some point in their lifetime.
- Small trees that cannot reach the sun because of the twisted or damaged larger trees tangled all around them. They require an outside force to clear away the damage or the small tree cannot develop properly. Like children growing up in a broken or abusive home, who need others to rescue them.
- Some glorious trees also bear fruit, providing food for the hungry. We should be sharing whatever food we have with the hungry and needy around us.
- Finally, notice the splendid, tall and majestic trees that shine in the sun providing shade for the overheated, shelter for the weary and home for the animals. Just as we Christians are to stand reaching for God and pointing the way for other to find Him! We are also called to provide shelter and rest for the weary travelers.
- What about Christmas trees?

Christmas is coming soon. What if you asked family to gather around their Christmas trees this year, read this story and choose one soul that they will pray for every time they see a tree this year? What if the next year when they gather around their Christmas trees, they celebrate the spiritual changes in the life of the person they prayed for all year, and then select another person for the coming year? What if they make it part of their annual family tradition? What kind of impact might that have on the kingdom heaven?

Well, there it is. My prayer that led me to a method of engaging families to pray together from the word trees. Isn't it amazing how God works in all things?

When I came home, I researched the word trees in the Bible and realized I can do a whole year's study on trees and their meaning!

And then…I shared the story with a few people, put it away…thought about it from time to time…and then life happened…and I forgot about it! I am as fickle as the Israelites-going from desperate for a word from God to failing to be obedient to follow through, in short order.

Back to the present. You will be happy to know that our God is a God of second chances and you can bet I will not waste my second chance. I will obediently complete my study on trees in the Bible and then share it with whomever and however I am led to. If God is not in it, count me out. I do not wish to stand alone in my pride any further or to ever forget the benefits and blessings of my God.

I have seen miracles unfold in this work. I was able to complete the first 202 verses of the King James Version with the word, tree, in just one week with commentary on each verse. I know for sure that I could not do this in my own power. In some of the Old Testament prophet sections, I would be working in the evening until my eyes crossed and saying, "God, I just don't understand this part. You are going to have to help me out here." The next morning, I got up worked my way through all the parables and visions in one day. It was like clarity was downloaded in my mind while I slept. Then, I had the internal drive to go back and add the verses with the plural trees.

I shared this story with my 3rd grade Sunday school class. They were in awe, but guess what they said. "Are you going to publish it?" My mouth dropped open for a minute and then I said "Yes?" kind of tentatively, which was met with roaring applause! Just sharing the journey with women has sparked some amazing changes in their journeys, as well. One rather introverted young lady, contacted me several times in one week to say she had been thinking about my "Trees" and she is writing a Bible study on fire. She wrote it, shared it with her small group after showing it to me. It was amazing and so professional. Her group said, "Wow, all year she didn't share or talk much. She was amazing." She will actually be sharing this study with a larger group of women in our church at the next Women's Breakfast. So, my desire for this project has been fulfilled before even publishing it. I owe grateful praise to the One who made it possible.

Each and every verse I completed drew me closer to knowing God more and His design and plan for us. I hope and pray it has the same effect on you as you read, study and meditate on it. I want you to catch a spark of joy in doing Bible study of your own. You only need, the Bible, pen and paper with a little quiet time and space. Any amount of time spent, will be blessed.

REVIEWS

Byron Brackett, Family Minister, Salem Baptist Church, "Renee, I am so glad that God put a book in your heart!"

Jessica Edwards, Revive Our Heart Ambassador, at the outset of the project. "Oh my, Renee! I love it that you love to study God's Word!!!! and how thorough you are! Trees are not something I have ever studied, at least not as a topic in the Bible... the judgment, the idolatry, the death, the strength, the blessing, the life associated with them."

Donna Darrah, Women's Ministry Team Leader, Salem Baptist Church, "God is going to use your writing, Renee. May God use your writing to draw many people's hearts to HIM!"

Amber Fletcher, Homeschool Mom, teaching her kids a Christian worldview, "Have you heard about the Aspen tree? All aspen trees come from one root. Just like Christ is the vine and we are the branches. We are to stay rooted in Christ, the Aspen trees are another created thing that in their design point to God."

Jessica Edwards, Revive Our Hearts Ambassador, at the end of phase one of the project, "Wow, there's so much there when everything the Bible says about trees is in one place. One thing that struck me was the very last verse you share from Revelation... it points back to the beginning, back to Genesis, and as you said, back to His original plan. What a picture of the sovereignty of God. He is in control, has been in control, and will continue to be in control! There is great comfort in that!"

ACKNOWLEDGEMENT

The source for all Scripture is King James Version

(Paraphrased to be understood by modern readers)

GENESIS

Genesis 1:11-12 And God said, Let the earth bring forth grass, the herb yielding seed, and fruit tree yielding fruit after his kind, whose seed is in itself, upon the earth: and it was so. And the earth brought forth grass, and herb yielding seed after his kind, and the tree yielding fruit, whose seed was in itself, after his kind: and God saw that it was good.

This is teaching us about reproduction, food and provision for the future creation of humans. The love of God is evident in that every single thing created before humans was for the pleasure and provision of them, as long as they are on the earth.

Genesis 1:29 And God said, Behold, I have given you every herb bearing seed, which is upon the face of all the earth, and every tree, in which is the fruit of a tree yielding seed; to you it shall be for food.

Here, we see food that replenishes itself by God's design.

Genesis 2:9 And out of the ground made the Lord God to grow every tree that is pleasant to the sight, and good for food; the tree of life, and also in the midst of the garden, and the tree of knowledge of good and evil.

Trees that provide food, life eternal and knowledge (both good and evil). Remember that Adam and Eve already had only knowledge of all that was good.

Genesis 2:16-17 And the Lord God commanded the man, saying, Of every tree of the garden you may freely eat: But of the tree of the knowledge of good and evil, you shall not eat of it: for in the day that you eat thereof you shall surely die.

There was only one test of obedience given to Adam and Eve.

Genesis 3:1-24 Now the serpent was more subtle than any beast of the field which the Lord God had made. And he said to the woman, Yes, has God said, "You shall not eat of every tree of the garden?" And the woman said to the serpent, "We may eat of the fruit of the trees of the garden: But of the fruit of the tree which is in the midst of the garden, God has said, You shall not eat of it, neither shall you touch it, lest you die." And the serpent said to the woman, "You shall not surely die: For God does know that in the day you eat of it, then your eyes shall be opened, and you shall be as gods, knowing good and evil." And when the woman saw that the tree was good for food, and that it was pleasant to the eyes, and a tree to be desired to make one wise, she took the fruit of it, and did eat, and gave some to her husband with her; and he did eat. And the eyes of them both were opened, and they knew that they were naked; and they sewed fig leaves together, and made themselves aprons. And they heard the voice of the Lord God walking in the garden in the cool of the day: and Adam and his wife hid themselves from the presence of the Lord God among the trees of the garden. And the Lord God called to Adam, and said to him, where are you? And he said, "I heard your voice in the garden, and I was afraid, because I was naked; and I hid myself." And he said, "Who told you that you are naked? Have you eaten of the tree that I commanded that you should not eat?" And the man said, "The woman whom You gave to be with me, she gave me of the tree, and I did eat." And the Lord God said to the woman, "What is this that you have done?" And the woman said, "The serpent beguiled me, and I did eat." And the Lord God said to the serpent, "Because you have done this, you are cursed above all cattle, and above every beast of the field; upon your belly shall you go, and dust shall you eat all the days of your life: And I will put enmity between you and the woman, and between your seed and her seed; it shall bruise your head, and you shall bruise his heel." To the woman he said, "I will greatly multiply your sorrow and your conception; in sorrow you shall bring forth children; and your desire shall be to your husband, and he shall rule over you." And to Adam he said, "Because you have listened to the voice of your wife, and have eaten of the tree, of which I commanded you, saying, you shall not eat of it: cursed is the ground for your sake; in sorrow shall you eat of it all the days of your life; Thorns also and thistles shall it bring forth to you; and you shall eat the herb of the field; In the sweat of your face shall you eat bread, till you return unto the ground; for out of it were you taken: for dust you are, and to dust you shall return." And Adam called his wife's name Eve; because she was the mother of all living. To Adam also and his wife did the Lord God make coats of skins, and clothed them.

And the Lord God said, "Behold, the man is become as one of us, to know good and evil: and now, lest he put forth his hand, and take also of the tree of life, and eat, and live forever." Therefore the Lord God sent him out from the garden of Eden, to till the ground that he was taken from. So, he drove out the man; and he placed at the east of the garden of Eden Cherubim, and a flaming sword which turned every way, to guard the way of the tree of life.

Come on now, Eve talking to a snake, really? I would run screaming just seeing a snake, much less having it speak to me. But I remember that Eve (and Adam) had only seen and known good things up to this point. This was their first encounter with evil. Women's fear of snakes came after the fall. Original sin came with a massive cost for all mankind. Because of Eve and Adam's lust of the eyes and disobedience, bitter consequences in the form of: separation from God, immediate spiritual death, cursed to eventual physical death by being banned from eating from the tree of life and being awakened to awareness of evil which resulted in loss of their purity. After the sin, this was the first instance of hiding in the trees, while thinking God can't see them there!

Genesis 18:4-8 "Let a little water, I pray you, be fetched, and wash your feet, and rest yourselves under the tree: And I will fetch a morsel of bread, and comfort your hearts; after that you shall pass on: for therefore are you come to your servant." And they said, "So do, as you have said." And Abraham hurried into the tent to Sarah, and said, "Make ready quickly three measures of fine meal, knead it, and make cakes upon the hearth." And Abraham ran to the herd, and fetched a calf tender and good, and gave it to a young man; and he hurried to dress it. And he took butter, and milk, and the calf which he had dressed, and set it before them; and he stood by them under the tree, and they did eat.

Here trees provided shade, a cooler air temperature, a comfortable place to rest, a sanctuary, food cooked over a wood fire for weary travelers.

Genesis 23:17-18a and the field of Ephron, which was in Machpelah, which was before Mamre, the field, and the cave which was in it, and all the trees that were in the field, that were in all the borders around it, were made sure unto Abraham for a possession.

Within Abraham's land that God had granted to him as a possession were included all the trees in the field and even the ones that were bordering it. Trees to provide for generations of his family for years to come. Trees that give protection, wood for building, fuel for burning, food (fruit, olives, figs), coolness of the shade-all are blessings from God. Have you ever thought to thank God for trees and all that they provide in your own life?

Genesis 30:37-43 And Jacob took him rods of green poplar, and of the hazel and chestnut tree; and cut white streaks in them, and made the white appear which was in the rods. And he set the rods which he had peeled before the flocks in the gutters in the watering troughs when the flocks came to drink, that they should conceive when they came to drink. And the flocks conceived before the rods, and brought forth cattle ring streaked, speckled, and spotted. And Jacob did separate the lambs, and set the faces of the flocks toward the ring streaked, and all the brown in the flock of Laban; and he put his own flocks by themselves, and put them not with Laban's cattle. And it came to pass, whenever the stronger cattle conceived, that Jacob laid the rods before the eyes of the cattle in the gutters, that they might conceive among the rods. But when the cattle were feeble, he did not put them in: so, the feebler were Laban's, and the stronger Jacob's. And the man increased exceedingly, and had much cattle, and maidservants, and menservants, and camels, and donkeys.

Jacob showed a particular type of wisdom in using branches of poplar, hazelnut and chestnut trees to settle the corrupt dealings of Laban by influencing the bearing of livestock in Jacob's favor. This brought provision and increase in wealth for Jacob.

Genesis 40:16-23 When the chief baker saw that the interpretation was good, he said to Joseph, I also was in my dream, and, behold, I had three white baskets on my head: And in the uppermost basket there was of all manner of baked goods for Pharaoh; and the birds did eat them out of the basket upon my head. And Joseph answered and said, this is the interpretation of that: The three baskets are three days: Yet within three days shall Pharaoh lift up your head from off you, and shall hang you on a tree; and the birds shall eat your flesh from off you.

And it came to pass the third day, which was Pharaoh's birthday, that he made a feast to all his servants: and he lifted up the head of the chief butler and the chief baker among his servants. And he restored the chief butler to his butlership again; and he gave the cup into Pharaoh's hand: But he hanged the chief baker: as Joseph had interpreted to them. Yet the chief butler did not remember Joseph, but forgot him.

Judgement for the chief baker occurred in the form of death, being hanged from a tree. Also, there was a broken promise of the butler (cup bearer) to remember Joseph.

EXODUS

Exodus 9:25 And the hail destroyed throughout all the land of Egypt all that was in the field, both man and beast; and the hail destroyed every herb of the field, and broke every tree of the field.

The Egyptian's initial judgement from God came in the form of loss of trees, which resulted in many losses: provision, food, comfort, shade, building material that would take many years to recover from.

Exodus 10:4-5 Else, if you refuse to let my people go, behold, tomorrow will I bring the locusts into your coast: And they shall cover the face of the earth, that one cannot be able to see the earth: and they shall eat the residue of that which is escaped, which remains to you from the hail, and shall eat every tree which grows for you out of the field:

The Egyptian's received increased consequences of judgement with each additional plague sent from God. The loss of the remaining trees that would take years to recover from resulting in famine.

Exodus 10:15 (Locusts) For they covered the face of the whole earth, so that the land was darkened; and they did eat every herb of the land, and all the fruit of the trees which the hail had left: and there remained not any green thing in the trees, or in the herbs of the field, through all the land of Egypt.

Pharaoh's hardened heart brought on the promised plague of God in the form of locusts destroying every green thing including all the trees. Devastation to the Egyptian way of life for a long time in the form of famine, lack of shade, lack of lumber for building.

Exodus 15:24-25 And the people murmured against Moses, saying, "What shall we drink?" And he cried to the Lord; and the Lord showed him a tree, which when he had cast into the waters, the waters were made sweet: there he made for them a statute and an ordinance, and there he proved them.

This was a testing of the Israelites faith in God's ability to provide for them with bitter waters. Their grumbling against Moses and his prayer for them was followed by supernatural provision of drinkable water. Once again, proving God's love for them.

Exodus 15:27 And they came to Elim, where there were twelve wells of water, and threescore (3X20=60) and ten palm trees: and they encamped there by the waters.

After testing the Israelites at Marah with bitter waters, now they are abundantly blessed with 12 wells of water and 70 palm trees for shade.

LEVITICUS

Leviticus 19:23 And when you come into the land, and shall have planted all manner of trees for food, then you shall count the fruit of the land as uncircumcised: three years shall it be as uncircumcised unto you: it shall not be eaten.

Once they reach the promised land and plant trees for food, the Israelites were instructed to wait for 3 years to eat the fruit of it because it is uncircumcised (unclean). This is another test of obedience.

Leviticus 23:40 And you shall take you on the first day the boughs of good trees, branches of palm trees, and the boughs of thick trees, and willows of the brook; and you shall rejoice before the Lord your God seven days.

Tree branches used in worship and rejoicing before the Lord God.

Leviticus 26:4 If you walk in my statutes, and keep my commandments, and do them; Then I will give you rain in due season, and the land shall yield her increase, and the trees of the field shall yield their fruit.

Being obedient to the law of the Lord comes with the promise of abundant blessing of rain to water the earth and plenty to eat.

Leviticus 26:20 And if you will not yet for all this listen to me, then I will punish you seven times more for your sins. And I will break the pride of your power; and I will make your heaven as iron, and your earth as brass: And your strength shall be spent in vain: for your land shall not yield her increase, neither shall the trees of the land yield their fruits.

The other side of the coin of God's blessing (Leviticus 26:4) for obedience is the promised punishment for ignoring God's law; 7 times the punishment, loss of power, everything feels like a heavy weight upon you, strength wasted on nothing, no food or fruit trees equals famine.

Leviticus 27:30 And all the tithe of the land, whether of the seed of the land, or of the fruit of the tree, is the Lord's: it is holy to the Lord.

This is instruction to show love being reciprocal to God by obedience in tithing (giving back a portion of what is already His that He has chosen to bless us with).

NUMBERS

Numbers 6:4 All the days of his separation shall he eat anything that is made of the vine tree, from the kernels even to the husk.

This is the Nazarite dedication and purification vow to follow the Lord in obedience all the days of his life. Nothing made of the vine tree, would signify no wine.

Numbers 24:6 As the valleys are, they spread forth, as gardens by the river's side, as the trees of lign aloes which the Lord has planted, and as cedar trees beside the waters.

Here we see a review of the view of the promised land, garden's well-watered by the rivers, lign Aloe trees are expensive, sweet-smelling wood and cedar trees are for building and making furniture.

Numbers 33:9 And they removed from Marah, and came unto Elim: and in Elim were twelve fountains of water, and threescore and ten palm trees; and they pitched there.

This is a review of their travels from Exodus, bitter waters made sweet followed by abundant blessing.

DEUTERONOMY

Deuteronomy 6:11 And houses full of all good things, which you did not fill, and wells dug, which you did not dig, vineyards and olive trees, which you did not plant; when you have eaten and be full.

The land the Israelites are being given has already got homes, wells, vineyards, olive trees and plenty to eat, without requiring the Israelites to labor for it. Wouldn't that be an awesome blessing for you and your family?

Deuteronomy 8:8 A land of wheat, and barley, and vines, and fig trees, and pomegranates; a land of olive oil, and honey;

This verse gives an additional description of how bountiful the land is.

Deuteronomy 12:2 You shall utterly destroy all the places, where the nations which you shall possess served their gods, upon the high mountains, and upon the hills, and under every green tree:

The Israelites are practicing false worship of idols in the shade of the exact same trees that God had created as a blessing for them. Total destruction is commanded.

Deuteronomy 16:21 You shall not plant yourself a grove of any kind of trees near the altar of the Lord your God, which you shall make for yourself.

A grove of trees near the altar of the Lord, would leave rotting fruit all around or people would be climbing in and around it to pick fruit, disrupting worship.

Deuteronomy 19:5 As when a man goes into the woods with his neighbor to cut wood, and his hand fetches a stroke with the axe to cut down the tree, and the head slips from the handle, and lights upon his neighbor, that he died; he shall flee unto one of those cities, and live.

When the accidental death of a neighbor while cutting down trees occurs, God provides a sanctuary city for the one holding the axe to be protected from vengeful family members.

Deuteronomy 20:19-20 When you shall besiege a city a long time, in making war against it to take it, you shall not destroy the trees there by forcing an axe against them: for you may eat of them, and you shall not cut them down (for the tree of the field is man's life) to employ them in the siege: Only the trees which you know that they be not trees for food, you shall destroy and cut them down; and you shall build bulwarks against the city that makes war with you, until it is subdued.

This appears to be instruction from God regarding which trees to use in battle and which to save along the lines of: In war, be thoughtful of which trees you cut down and do not spite yourself by destroying the trees that will provide food and blessing for years to come.

Deuteronomy 21:22-23 And if a man has committed a sin worthy of death, and he is to be put to death, and you hang him on a tree: His body shall not remain all night upon the tree, but you shall bury him that day; (for he that is hanged is accursed of God;)

We get a description of judgement for a sin worthy of death. The person will be hung from a tree, left hanging until evening as a warning example to others, and then buried that same day before the sun goes down.

Deuteronomy 22:6 If a bird's nest chance to be before you in the way in any tree, or on the ground, whether they be young ones, or eggs, and the mother bird is sitting upon the young, or upon the eggs, you shall not take the mother with the young.

This shows respect for nature and the reproduction of the mother to provide more eggs.

Deuteronomy 24:20 When you beat your olive tree, you shall not go over the boughs again: it will be for the stranger, the fatherless, and the widow.

Here we see provision commanded to be left behind for the orphans and the widows, olives and olive oil for fuel and for food.

Deuteronomy 28:40-42 You shall have olive trees throughout all your coasts, but you shall not anoint yourself with the oil; for your olive shall cast his fruit. You shall have sons and daughters, but you shall not enjoy them; for they shall go into captivity. All your trees and fruit of your land shall the locust consume.

Olive trees are a sign of God's blessed abundance to the Israelites, but He is warning them that they may own the trees and see them, as well as have children, but they will not enjoy any of it. It speaks of judgement in the form of children taken captive and all trees and fruit eaten by locusts leading to famine.

Deuteronomy 34:2-4 And the Lord showed him (Moses) all the land of Gilead, to Dan, And all Naphtali, and the land of Ephraim, and Manasseh, and all the land of Judah, to the utmost sea, And the south, and the plain of the valley of Jericho, the city of palm trees, unto Zoar. And the Lord said to him, this is the land which I swore to Abraham, Isaac, and Jacob, saying, I will give it to your seed: I have caused you to see it with your eyes, but you shall not go over there.

The city of palm trees is mentioned in the middle of Moses view of the Promised Land near the end of his life. Jericho is the city of palms. The writer of Deuteronomy chose to describe it as the city of palm trees, Perhaps the palm trees were of more value than the people living there and their sinful choices?

JOSHUA

Joshua 8:29 And the king of Ai he hanged on a tree until evening: and as soon as the sun was down, Joshua commanded that they should take his carcass down from the tree, and cast it at the entrance of the gate of the city, and raise on it a great heap of stones, that remains to this day. We learn of judgement, hanging, followed by mercy burial, in obedience to earlier instruction regarding hanging, plus a monument as a reminder of the story.

Joshua 10:23-27 And they did so, and brought forth those five kings to him out of the cave, the king of Jerusalem, the king of Hebron, the king of Jarmuth, the king of Lachish, and the king of Eglon. And, when they brought out those kings to Joshua, he called for all the men of Israel, and said to the captains of the men of war which went with him, come near, put your feet upon the necks of these kings. And they came near, and put their feet upon the necks of them. And Joshua said to them, Fear not, nor be dismayed, be strong and of good courage: for thus shall the Lord do to all your enemies against whom you fight. And afterward Joshua beat them, and killed them, and hung them on five trees: and they were hanging upon the trees until the evening. And at the going down of the sun, that Joshua commanded, and they took them down off the trees, and cast them into the cave where they had been hiding, and laid great stones in the cave's mouth, which remain until this very day. The hanging execution of the enemies of both Israel and God. But Joshua still showing respect to God by taking them down from the trees at night and burying the bodies in a cave.

JUDGES

Judges 1:16 And the children of the Kenite, Moses' father-in law, went up out of the city of palm trees (Jericho) with the children of Judah into the wilderness of Judah, which lies in the south of Arad; and they went and dwelt among the people.

The city of palm trees is mentioned again.

Judges 3:13 And he gathered unto him the children of Ammon and Amalek, and went and smote Israel, and possessed the city of palm trees (Jericho).

The city of palm trees is mentioned again. This must have been a city known as the city of palm trees because of either the abundance of palm trees there or the quality of the palm trees growing there.

Judges 4:5 And she dwelt under the palm tree of Deborah between Ramah and Bethel in mount Ephraim: and the children of Israel came up to her for judgment.

Deborah in her wisdom chose to do her judgement in a meeting place in the cool shade of a tree.

Judges 9:7-15 And when they told it to Jotham, he went and stood in the top of mount Gerizim, and lifted up his voice, and cried, and said to them, listen to me, you men of Shechem, that God may listen to you. The trees went forth on a time to anoint a king over them; and they said to the olive tree, "Reign over us." But the olive tree said to them, "Should I leave my fatness, wherewith by me they honor God and man, and go to be promoted over the trees?" And the trees said to the fig tree, "Come, and reign over us." But the fig tree said to them, "Should I forsake my sweetness, and my good fruit, and go to be promoted over the trees?" Then said the trees to the vine, "Come, and reign over us."

And the vine said to them, "Should I leave my wine, which cheers God and man, and go to be promoted over the trees?" Then said all the trees to the bramble, "Come, and reign over us." And the bramble said to the trees, "If in truth you anoint me king over you, then come and put your trust in my shadow: and if not, let fire come out of the bramble, and devour the cedars of Lebanon."

Appointed king of the trees-the bramble, nominated by the other trees, not by God. All the other trees approached chose to continue to do their own assigned task to honor God, but the bramble rose up and exalted himself with a threat and promise to burn and devour all who did not put their trust in him, an indication of Satan in his pride, perhaps?

1 SAMUEL

1 Samuel 14:2 And Saul tarried in the uttermost part of Gibeah under a pomegranate tree which is in Migron: and the people that were with him were about six hundred men;

These trees provided rest, shade, refreshment for this gathering of men, the army of Saul.

1 Samuel 22:6 When Saul heard that David was discovered, and the men that were with him, (now Saul abode in Gibeah under a tree in Ramah, having his spear in his hand, and all his servants were standing about him;)

Saul, once again, resting under a tree while all of his soldiers are searching for David shows a lack of character.

1 Samuel 31:11-13 And when the inhabitants of Jabeshgilead heard of what the Philistines had done to Saul; All the valiant men arose, and went all night, and took the body of Saul and the bodies of his sons from the wall of Bethshan, and came to Jabesh, and burnt them there. And they took their bones, and buried them under a tree at Jabesh, and fasted for seven days.

Saul had been appointed by God (1 Samuel 9:15-20) and deserving of the honor of a proper burial with his sons. He was buried under at tree at Jabesh. Saul had in life had a habit of resting in the shade of trees. It is fitting that this final resting place be under a tree.

2 SAMUEL

2 Samuel 5:11 And Hiram king of Tyre sent messengers to David, and cedar trees, and carpenters, and masons: and they built David a house.

What an amazing gift from King Hiram to King David, not only cedar trees, but carpenters and masons to build David's house as well! This confirmed for David God's blessing on him and he worshipped and praised God for the gift!

2 Samuel 5:23-24 And when David enquired of the Lord, he said, you shall not go up; but fetch a compass behind them, and come upon them over against the mulberry trees. And let it be, when you hear the sound of a going in the tops of the mulberry trees, that then you shall stir yourself: for then shall the Lord go out before you, to smite the host of the Philistines.

The location for a victorious battle defined, by the Lord, as against the mulberry (or balsam) trees. The signal for the battle the wind stirring the tops of the trees, sounding like marching. These were specific directions for David to follow in a display of full obedience to God. It will prove to gain him the victory.

1 KINGS

1 Kings 4:25 And Judah and Israel dwelt safely, every man under his vine and under his fig tree, from Dan to Beersheba, all the days of Solomon.

These are symbols of abundant blessing of God, each has his own tree and vine.

1 Kings 4:33 And he spoke of trees, from the cedar tree that is in Lebanon even to the hyssop that springs out of the wall: he spoke also of beasts, and fowl, and creeping things, and fish.

We get a glimpse of Solomon's wisdom in all things including God's design of the natural world.

1Kings 5:6-12 Now I command you that they cut me cedar trees out of Lebanon; and my servants shall be with your servants: and to you I will give payment for your servants according to all that you shall appoint: for you know that there is not among us any that can skill to cut timber like unto the Sidonians. And it happened, when Hiram heard the words of Solomon, that he rejoiced greatly, and said, blessed be the Lord this day, which has given unto David a wise son over this great people. And Hiram sent to Solomon, saying, I have considered the things which you sent to me for: and I will do all you desire concerning timber of cedar, and concerning timber of fir. My servants shall bring them down from Lebanon to the sea: and I will convey them by sea in floats to the place that you shall appoint me, and will cause them to be discharged there, and you shall receive them: and you shall accomplish my desire, in giving food for my household. So, Hiram gave Solomon cedar trees and fir trees according to all his desire. And Solomon gave Hiram twenty thousand measures of wheat for food to his household, and twenty measures of pure oil: thus, gave Solomon to Hiram year by year. And the Lord gave Solomon wisdom, as he promised him: and there was peace between Hiram and Solomon; and they two made a league together.

King Hiram was a wise king, who loved King David, and recognized King Solomon's wisdom. Hiram thanked God for blessing David with a wise son to rule this great people, the Israelites. He again blessed Solomon even more than he had blessed his father, David. He gave him not only timber (cedar and fir), but also had floats built to send it to him. Solomon repaid the blessing with an abundance of wheat and oil and continued giving every year. The result was peace between their nations.

1 Kings 6:23 And within the oracle he made two cherubim of olive tree, each ten cubits high.

The strength of the olive wood and its abundant availability resulted in its being used to create items of worship to God, Cherubim specifically.

1 Kings 6:29-31 And he carved all the walls of the house around with carved figures of cherubim and palm trees and open flowers, inside and out. And the floor of the house he overlaid with gold, inside and out. And for the entering of the oracle, he made doors of olive tree: the lintel and side posts were a fifth part of the wall. The two doors also were of olive tree; and he carved upon them carvings of cherubim and palm trees and open flowers, and overlaid them with gold, and spread gold upon the cherubim, and upon the palm trees. So also made he for the door of the temple posts of olive tree, a fourth part of the wall. And the two doors were of fir tree: the two leaves of the one door were folding, and the two leaves of the other door were folding. And he carved on them cherubim and palm trees and open flowers: and covered them with gold fitted upon the carved work. And he built the inner court with three rows of cut stone, and a row of cedar beams.

God gave specific instructions to Solomon (1 Kings 5:1- 6:38) for building His temple (home on the earth in the Old Testament) included many types of trees in the building and decorating. Olive trees should be used for the doors and door frames. Two folding doors to be made of fir. A row of cedar beams created some of the inner court, Palm trees were carved in the olive wood for decoration (along with some additional images) overlaid with gold. The very detail and intricacy of the design shows the creativity of the Creator and the need for obedience of the builders. The finished temple had to be the grandest building ever built on the face of the earth. Just thinking about it and trying to envision this temple brings awe of God's majesty.

1 Kings 6:31-36 And for the entering of the oracle he made doors of olive tree: the lintel and side posts were a fifth part of the wall. The two doors were also of olive tree; and he carved on them carvings of cherubim and palm trees and open flowers, and overlaid them with gold, and spread gold upon the cherubim, and on the palm trees. So also, he made for the door of the temple posts of olive tree, a fourth part of the wall. And the two doors were of fir tree: the two leaves of the one door were folding, and the two leaves of the other door were folding. And he carved cherubim and palm trees and open flowers: and covered them with gold fitted upon the carved work. And he built the inner court with three rows of hewed stone, and a row of cedar beams.

Certain trees used in the building of God's house at God's command and very specific instruction from the perspective of the author of 1 Kings. (Jeremiah according to tradition).

1 Kings 7:36 For on the plates of the ledges of it (the stands of the water basins; called the sea in the temple), and on the borders of it, he graved cherubim, lions, and palm trees, according to the proportion of every one, and additions round about.

These are more very specific instruction of what to decorate the stands in God's temple with and also how to make the cherubim, lions and palm trees proportionate in size. How would they know the proportion of the cherubim, if they had not seen them? By God's instruction! This is told from the perspective of the author of 1 Kings. (Jeremiah according to tradition).

1 Kings 9:10-11 And it was at the end of twenty years, when Solomon had built the two houses, the house of the Lord, and the king's house, (Now Hiram the king of Tyre had furnished Solomon with cedar trees and fir trees, and with gold, according to all his desire,) that then King Solomon gave Hiram twenty cities in the land of Galilee.

King Solomon, in his wisdom, repaid King Hiram's blessing of cedar and fir trees and gold across twenty years of building both God's house (temple) and Solomon's house (palace) with not only initial payment of wheat and oil, plus annual gifts, but also twenty cities in the land of Galilee.

1 Kings 10:11-12 And the navy also of Hiram, that brought gold from Ophir, brought in from Ophir great plenty of almug trees, and precious stones. And the king made of the almug trees pillars for the house of the Lord, and for the king's house, harps also and psalteries for singers: there came no such almug trees, nor were seen unto this day.

They must have used almost every almug tree as pillars for the house of the Lord and for King Solomon's house. They also made harps and psalteries for worship of the One True God from the abundance of almug trees.

1 Kings 10:27 And the king made silver as common in Jerusalem as stones, and cedars made he as plentiful as the sycamore trees that are in the vale, for abundance.

Solomon imported and abundance of both silver and cedar trees to Jerusalem. Cedar was considered the best wood for building, perhaps because of its fragrance.

1 Kings 14:23 For they also built them high places, and images, and groves, on every high hill, and under every green tree.

The excessive places of false worship to idols built by the wayward Israelites under every tree are a direct insult to God.

1 Kings 19:4-5 But he himself went a day's journey into the wilderness, and came and sat down under a juniper tree: and he requested for himself that he might die; and said, "It is enough; now, O Lord, take away my life; for I am not better than my fathers." And as he lay and slept under a juniper tree, behold, then an angel touched him, and said to him, Arise and eat. Elijah hiding in fear from Jezebel wishing to die in the shade of a juniper tree (1 Kings 1:2).

His being in the shade shows that he still cares about his own comfort, even though distressed exceedingly to the point of wishing for death. God provided Elijah with rest, comfort, food, safety until he recovered.

2 KINGS

2 Kings 3:19 And you shall destroy every fenced city, and every choice city, and shall cut down every good tree, and stop up all wells of water, and cover every good piece of land with stones.

Elisha gives instruction of the Lord in a battle against the Moabites to destroy every good tree, which has implications of future loss of provision.

2 Kings 3:25 And they (Moabites) beat down the cities, and on every good piece of land cast every man his stone, and filled it; and they stopped all the wells of water, and felled all the good trees: only in Kirharaseth left they the stones thereof; this is how the slingers went about it, and struck it.

The kings of Israel, Judah and Edom made a pact to fight a battle together, leaving out the most important thing that they needed, God. God's judgement came in the form of Moabites descending on their land and destroying it utterly. Cutting down all the good trees has a long-lasting curse of heat from lack of shade, loss of food supply from the fruit of the trees, animals leaving because they have no place to rest or make homes.

2 Kings 16:4 And he sacrificed and burnt incense in the high places, and on the hills, and under every green tree.

Ahaz' sin against God is displayed by his idol worship under every green tree.

2 Kings 17:10 And they set them up images and groves in every high hill, and under every green tree.

Israel's sin is repeated- excessive idol worship under every green tree.

2 Kings 18:31 Listen not to Hezekiah: for the king of Assyria says, Make an agreement with me by a present, and come to me, and then eat every man of his own vine, and of his own fig tree, and drink every one the waters of his own well:

This is a promise of abundance from the Assyrian king, not from God. He seems to be mocking God's earlier promise of abundant blessing.

2 Kings 19:23 By your messengers you have mocked the Lord, and have said, "With the multitude of my chariots I am come up to the height of the mountains, to the far recesses of Lebanon, and will cut down the tall cedar trees of it, and the choice fir trees (cypresses) of it: and I will enter into the lodgings of his borders, and into the most fruitful forest of his Carmel.

Sennacherib, King of Assyria, thinks he can just waltz in and destroy Israel's cedar and fir trees and the most fruitful forest in it, as well. The brazen statements made here prove to be his downfall, when God chooses to show him who is really in charge by protecting Jerusalem (because of God's promise to David (2 Kings 19:31-34) "They will not release an arrow in this city and will return the way they came in defeat.")

1 CHRONICLES

1 Chronicles 14:14-15 Therefore David enquired again of God; and God said to him, do not go not up after them; turn away from them, and come upon them over against the mulberry trees. And it shall be, when you shall hear a sound of going in the tops of the mulberry trees (as marching), that then you shall go out to battle: for God is gone before you to smite the host of the Philistines. David therefore did as God commanded him:

A repeated telling of this story from 2 Samuel 5:23-24, with the addition of David's obedience to God.

1 Chronicles 16:33 Then shall the trees of the woods sing out at the presence of the Lord, because he comes to judge the earth.

Wow, the trees will sing out when the Lord comes to judge the earth- incredible!

1 Chronicles 22:4 Also cedar trees in abundance: for the Zidonians (Sidonians) and they of Tyre brought much cedar wood to David.

This is a reference to 2 Samuel 5:11, When King Hiram sent David wood and carpenters and masons from Sidonia to build his home.

1 Chronicles 27:28 And over the olive trees and the sycamore trees that were in the low plains was Baalhanan.

This reference is to part of a counting and division of all things in the land that belonged to King David and appointing stewards over it all. Trees are included in the things that need to be stewarded because of their great value and provision for people.

2 CHRONICLES

2 Chronicles 1:15 And the king made silver and gold at Jerusalem as plenteous as stones, and cedar trees made he as the sycamore trees that are in the vale for abundance the Gederite: and over the cellars of oil was Joash.

Here is a retelling of the story in 1 Kings 10:27 with the addition of Joash being in charge of the cellars of oil.

2 Chronicles 2:8-9 Send me also cedar trees, fir trees, and algum trees, out of Lebanon: for I know that your servants are the most skilled to cut timber in Lebanon; and, behold, my servants shall be with your servants, Even to prepare me timber in abundance: for the house which I am about to build shall be wonderful great.

This is a retelling of Solomon's request to King Hiram of Sidonia 1Kings 5:6-12 with the added description of "the house I am about to build shall be wonderful-great." This shows that Solomon had already received the instruction of exactly how to build God's house directly from God (1 Kings 5:1- 6:38) and King Solomon was both excited and amazed!

2 Chronicles 3:5 And the greater house he made the ceiling with fir tree, which he overlaid with fine gold, and set palm trees and chains on it.

Solomon builds the house of God in worship to God, showing obedience in following specific instructions.

2 Chronicles 9:10-11 And the servants also of Huram (Hiram), and the servants of Solomon, which brought gold from Ophir, brought algum trees and precious stones. And the king made of the algum trees terraces to the house of the Lord, and to the king's palace, and harps and psalteries for singers: and there were none such seen before in the land of Judah.

This chronicles a retelling of the story in 1 Kings 10:11-12.

2 Chronicles 9:27 And the king made silver in Jerusalem as stones, and cedar trees made he as the sycamore trees that are in the low plains in abundance.

We see a retelling of both 1 Kings 10:27 and 2 Chronicles 1:15

2 Chronicles 28:4 He also sacrificed and burned incense in the high places, and on the hills, and under every green tree.

Ahaz' grievous sin is documented again

2 Chronicles 28:15 And the men who have been mentioned by name arose, and took the captives, and with the spoil clothed all that were naked among them, and arrayed them, and put sandals on them, and gave them to eat and drink, and anointed them, and carried all the feeble of them upon donkeys, and brought them back to their kinfolk at Jericho, the city of palm trees, to their brethren: then they returned to Samaria.

The men mentioned are certain chiefs of Ephraim. The setting was the army of Judah was coming back from attacking the Israelites and killing many of them with spoils of war and prisoners to make slaves. When they arrived at Samaria expecting congratulations and celebration for what they had done, they were instead corrected by Obed, a prophet of the Lord. Upon hearing the judgement, some chiefs of Ephraim (not wanting to be associated with their guilt) tried to correct the situation in the eyes of the Lord by clothing, feeding, giving drink and putting sandals on the feet of the prisoners. They then took them all back to their family in Jericho, the city of palm trees.

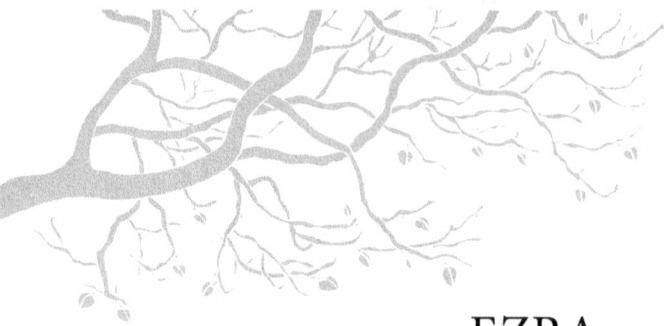

EZRA

Ezra 3:7 They gave money to the masons, and carpenters; and food, and drink, and oil, to them of Zidon (Sidonia), and to them of Tyre, to bring cedar trees from Lebanon to the sea of Joppa, according to the grant that they had of Cyrus, King of Persia. This is the second time that the Sidonians sent masons, and carpenters and lumber to build the temple of God.

This time was rebuilding it after it being destroyed. Tyre was mentioned in helping this time as well and payment was made with the kings of both Sidonia and Tyre, but the payment was made by King Cyrus of Persia in a grant. This is more evidence that God truly does have control of even pagan earthly kings and kingdoms.

NEHEMIAH

Nehemiah 8:15 And that they should publish and proclaim in all their cities, and in Jerusalem, saying, go forth to the mountain, and fetch olive branches, and pine branches, and myrtle branches, and palm branches, and branches of thick trees, to make booths, as it is written.

These are instructions for the Festival of Booths, 7 days of worshipping God and the reading of God's Word, while camping in a booth made of tree branches near or on top of their homes. This ritual seems to be taking the Israelites out of their comfort zones to have a better focus on God in worship and more focus on hearing His Word.

Nehemiah 9:25 And they took strong cities, and a fat land, and possessed houses full of all goods, wells dug, vineyards, and olive yards, and fruit trees in abundance: so, they ate, and were filled, and became fat, and delighted themselves in His great goodness.

Nehemiah was reading from God's Word to remind the Israelites what God had done in the history of their people. Coming into the promised land that was so abundantly rich in all they needed to live: houses full of furnishings, wells already dug, mature vineyards, olive groves and fruit orchards. The Israelites ate until filled and then became fat living on the fat of the land, they took delight in God's goodness. However, in the very next verse they turned away from God again, feeling very self-sufficient.

Nehemiah 10:35-37 And to bring the first fruits of our ground, and the first fruits of all fruit of all trees, year by year, into the house of the Lord: Also the firstborn of our sons, and of our cattle, as it is written in the law, and the firstlings of our herds and of our flocks, to bring to the house of our God, unto the priests that minister in the house of our God: And that we should bring the first fruits of our dough, and our offerings, and the fruit of all manner of trees, of wine and oil, to the priests, to the chambers of the house of our God; and the tithes of our ground unto the Levites, that the same Levites might have the tithes in all the cities of our farming.

This gives instruction about tithing on all the things that God blesses us with, for us to remember WHO the blessings came from. Tithe on all garden goods, all fruit from trees, first born sons, firstborn cattle, herds, and flocks, wheat and grain products, offerings, wine and oil. God does not need our tithes. The tithes were established as a reminder to us and used to support the priests and now the church and her mission.

ESTHER

Esther 2:21-23 In those days, while Mordecai sat in the king's gate, two of the king's chamberlains, Bigthan and Teresh, which kept the door, were angry, and sought to lay hands on the king Ahasuerus. And this was known to Mordecai, who told it to Esther the queen; and Esther told the king of it in Mordecai's name. And when inquisition was made of the matter, it was found true; therefore, they were both hanged on a tree: and it was written in the book of the chronicles before the king.

This speaks of judgement of the king's chamberlains and their well-deserved punishment, to be hung on a tree for their deception.

JOB

Job 14:7-10 For there is hope of a tree, if it be cut down, it will sprout again, and that the tender branch of it will not cease. Though the root of it wax old in the earth, and the stock of it die in the ground; Yet through the scent of water it will bud, and bring forth boughs like a plant. But man dies, and wastes away: yes, man gives up the ghost and, where is he?

Hope of rebirth, renewal and fresh purity forms a tender heart, as long as we are rooted in Christ, fresh water (even the scent of it) brings forth the buds that will bloom into new life.

Job 19:10 He has destroyed me on every side, and I am gone: and my hope has He removed like a tree.

Comparing hopelessness of Job to a tree utterly destroyed, root and all! If the root is destroyed the tree can never again bud or blossom or return to life.

Job 24:20 The womb shall forget him; the worm shall feed sweetly on him he shall be no more remembered; and wickedness shall be broken as a tree.

Even a broken tree can be renewed, saved, (as long as it has a good root) but the wickedness must be broken.

Job 40:21-22 He lay under the shady trees, in the covert of the reed, and fens. The shady trees cover him with their shadow; the willows of the brook compass him about.

This is speaking of the Behemoth. He is so large that he pretty much does and lays wherever he wishes. Shade trees are an excellent resting place to escape the heat of the day.

PSALM

Psalm 1:3 And he shall be like a tree planted by the rivers of water, that brings forth His fruit in His season; His leaf shall not wither; and whatever he does shall prosper.

He who delights in the law of the Lord and keeps his root in the water (studies God's Word), is then refreshed and brings fruit (guides others to Salvation in Christ and increases in the fruit of the Spirit personally), in season (God's not our own), keeping connected in Christ. We will not grow too tired even in old age to press on in service. Our service to God will prosper for His kingdom.

Psalm 37:35-36 And I have seen the wicked in great power, and spreading himself like a green bay tree. Yet he passed away, and, then, he was not: yes, I sought him, but he could not be found.

Even though the wicked seem to prosper for a season, when they are gone, they are truly and eternally gone without hope.

Psalm 52:8 But I am like a green olive tree in the house of God: I trust in the mercy of God for ever and ever.

Olive trees bear such a place of honor and value. They are used for food, fuel, building the house of God here on earth. Green represents maintaining our youthful outlook and energy, God's mercy and love will always be enough to renew us.

Psalm 74:5 A man was famous because he had lifted up axes upon the thick trees. But now they break down the carved work of it at once with axes and hammers. They have set fire to God's sanctuary; they have defiled by casting down the dwelling place of His name to the ground.

Men were once famous for being good at chopping down trees and the ability to carve beautiful decorations from them. But then they used to the axes and hammers to destroy the carved work that decorated God's temple and then they set fire to it. They went so far as to burn God's temple to the ground.

Psalm 78:47 He destroyed their vines with hail, and their sycamore trees with frost.

This shows another small part of judgement for turning away from God through the destroying of vines and trees by natural forces (hail and frost). This had lasting effects of removing all the blessings He had provided through them.

Psalm 92:12-14 The righteous shall flourish like the palm tree: he shall grow like a cedar in Lebanon. Those that are planted in the house of the Lord shall flourish in the courts of our God. They shall still bring forth fruit in old age; they shall be fat and flourishing;

This is a repeat of everything we already heard in Psalms about promises of flourishing, growth, strength, when we choose to remain planted in the house of the Lord and will flourish in the courts of God, even in old age.

Psalm 96:12-13 Let the field be joyful, and all that is in it: then shall all the trees of the wood rejoice before the Lord: for he comes to judge the earth: he shall judge the world with righteousness, and the people with his truth.

The trees rejoicing before the Lord when He comes to judge the earth, an earlier verse mentioned the trees singing when He comes to judge.

Psalm 104:16-17 The trees of the Lord are full of sap; the cedars of Lebanon, which he has planted; Where the birds make their nests: as for the stork, the fir trees are her house.

Oh, that we as Christians would be full of sap, blooming where we are planted by the Lord and being a sanctuary for those in need.

Psalm 105:33 He smote their vines also and their fig trees; and broke the trees of their coasts.

This is speaking of the plagues on the Egyptians.

Psalm 148:9 Mountains, and all hills; fruitful trees, and all cedars:

This is in the midst of a retelling of all things God created for humans to survive and thrive on earth, by David (Psalm 148:1-14).

PROVERBS

Proverbs 3:18 She is a tree of life to them that lay hold upon her: and happy is every one that retains her.

Wisdom is our tree of life. The more we reach for God's wisdom and hold onto it the happier we will be.

Proverbs 11:30 The fruit of the righteous is a tree of life; and he that wins souls is wise.

and happy is every one that retains her (wisdom).

We require a repeat of Proverbs 3:18, because we usually do not get it the first time, with the added promise of winning souls-Amazing.

Proverbs 13:12 Hope deferred makes the heart sick: but when the desire comes, it is a tree of life.

Waiting for whatever we hope for can be sad and very distressing, but when our hope is finally realized it is like renewed joy in life.

Proverbs 15:4 A wholesome tongue is a tree of life: but perverseness in our speech is a breach in the spirit.

We are told to speak only life-giving words, words that cause harm to others will cause trouble in your spirit and in your walk with God.

Proverbs 27:18 Whoever keeps the fig tree shall eat the fruit of it: so, he that waits on his master shall be honored.

Just as a fruit bearing tree has to be cultivated to continue bearing fruit, our relationship with God has to be cultivated. This is how we honor our Master.

ECCLESIASTES

Ecclesiastes 2:5-6 I made me gardens and orchards, and I planted trees in them of all kinds of fruits: I made me pools of water, to water the wood that brings forth trees:

Solomon in old age is recalling the "I did for me things of his life" and even neglecting to say that God gave him the wisdom to do it all and be successful.

Ecclesiastes 11:3 If the clouds are full of rain, they empty themselves on the earth: and if the tree falls toward the south, or the north, in the place where the tree falls, there it shall:

Be a blessing, when your cup is full share with others. Wherever you happen to be, be a blessing, God has providently placed you where you landed.

Ecclesiastes 12:5 Also when they are afraid of heights, and fears are in the way, and the almond tree flourishes, and the grasshopper is a burden too heavy to bear itself, and desire fails: because man is going to his final home, and the mourners go around the streets:

Waiting until the sorrows of life and the end comes is not the plan, we are to consider our sins until we come to repentance. We are to think of how we have wronged God as we go along, not only reaching for God when the going gets tough.

SONG OF SONGS

Song of Songs 2:3 As the apple tree among the trees of the wood, so is my beloved among the sons. I sat down under his shadow with great delight, and his fruit was sweet to my taste.

This is a picture of the passionate love we should have for Christ. He is our beloved, the apple of our eye, under His shadow is great delight.

Song of Songs 2:13 The fig tree puts forth her green figs, and the vines with the tender grapes give a good smell. Arise, my love, my fair one, and come away.

Green figs bear the promise of ripened fruit in the future, the aroma of things growing from the earth bear promise. Arise, beloved and come to Christ.

Song of Songs 4:13-14 Your plants are an orchard of pomegranates, with pleasant fruits; camphire, with spikenard, spikenard and saffron; calamus and cinnamon, with all trees of frankincense; myrrh and aloes, with all the chief spices:

This speaks of so many things that God had created with a pleasant aroma and some even have healing or restorative powers for people. Solomon comparing these things to his love.

Song of Songs 7:7-8 This your stature is likened to a palm tree, and thy breasts to clusters of grapes. I said, I will go up to the palm tree, I will take hold of the boughs of: now also your breasts shall be as clusters of the vine, and the smell of thy nose like apples;

Strength of stature would represent steadfastness. A woman's breast is actually food to her young by God's design. Approach and hold onto Christ's strength and enjoy the aroma of a blessed life.

Song of Songs 8:5 Who is this that comes up from the wilderness, leaning upon her beloved?

I raised you up under the apple tree: there your mother brought you forth: there she gave you birth.

Here is A word picture of a prodigal child returning home leaning upon their beloved Christ as they are returning home to the shade of the very apple tree they were born and raised under.

ISAIAH

Isaiah 6:13 But yet in it shall be a tenth, and it shall return, and shall be eaten: as a teil tree, and as an oak, whose substance is in them, when they cast their leaves: so, the holy seed shall be the substance thereof.

When Christians cast their leaves, they scatter seeds to salvation. The return of even a tenth of the seed rooting and growing to maturity makes the scattering well worth the effort.

Isaiah 7:2 And it was told the house of David, saying, Syria is confederate with Ephraim. And his heart was moved, and the heart of his people, as the trees of the wood are moved with the wind.

It was a time of war and an Israelite tribe Ephraim partnered with their Syrian enemies. They had been holding them off up to this point and this added support and manpower brought fear into the hearts of David and the people. It washed over them like the wind blowing through the trees.

Isaiah 10:19 And the rest of the trees of his forest shall be few, that a child may write them.

This is comparing the remnant of Israel that will be left. Such a small number of trees will be left in the forest that a child could count them.

Isaiah 14:8 Yes, the fir trees rejoice at You, and the cedars of Lebanon, saying, Since You are laid down, no one can come against us.

This appears to be speaking of the trees rejoicing again over Jesus, laying down His life, to win the victory over sin, that no one can come against us.

Isaiah 17:6 Yet gleaning grapes shall be left in it, as the shaking of an olive tree, two or three berries in the top of the uppermost bough, four or five in the outmost fruitful branches thereof, says the Lord God of Israel.

Leaving the most fruitful branches represents mature and fruitful Christians left on earth to continue yielding for God's kingdom.

Isaiah 24:13 When thus it shall be in the midst of the land among the people, there shall be as the shaking of an olive tree, and as the gleaning grapes when the vintage is done.

This is the final harvest of souls when all the work on earth for God's glory is done.

Isaiah 34:3 And all the host of heaven shall be dissolved, and the heavens shall be rolled together as a scroll: and all their host shall fall down, as the leaf falls off from the vine, as a falling fig from the fig tree.

This word picture is literally the sky being rolled back as a scroll, stars falling from the sky just as fruit and leaves fall to the ground and Heaven in its entirety being revealed to all.

Isaiah 36:16 Listen not to Hezekiah: said the king of Assyria, make an agreement with me by a present, and come out to me: and eat each and every one of his own vines, and every one of his own fig trees, and drink every one the waters of his own cistern.

We have a repeat of the promise of blessing and abundance to all from the king of Assyria, not from God, to all who will not listen to God's appointed prophet.

Isaiah 37:24 By your servants have you reproached the Lord, and said, By the multitude of my chariots am I come up to the height of the mountains, to the sides of Lebanon; and I will cut down the tall cedars there, and the choice fir trees there: and I will enter into the height of his border, and the forest of his Carmel.

Isaiah gives a repeat of the level of pride of Sennacherib, King of Assyria, in thinking he can march his army in and defeat Israel. Threatening to cut down the tall cedars and the best fir trees could be literal or a representation of cutting down the strongest and best soldiers of the Israelites.

Isaiah 40:20 He that is so impoverished that he has no oblation (offering to God) chooses a tree that will not rot; he seeks to him a cunning workman to prepare a graven image that shall not be moved.

False worship of tree carvings crafted to look like something more and better from a piece of wood. They think it will not rot, however, it will. The craftsman makes this to be his offering to his version of a god.

Isaiah 41:19 I will plant in the wilderness the cedar, the shittah tree, and the myrtle, and the oil tree; I will set in the desert the fir tree, and the pine, and the box tree together: That they may see, and know, and consider, and understand together, that the hand of the Lord has done this, and the Holy One of Israel has created it.

The Holy One, the Lord is the only one ever or since with the power to grow a variety of trees in the desert. All who see it will stand in awe of His power over all things. They will know, consider and understand Him better through this experience.

Isaiah 44:14 He cuts down cedars, and takes the cypress and the oak, which he strengthens for himself among the trees of the forest: he plants an ash, and the rain nourishes it.

This is speaking of the person in the next verses. He takes down many mature and useful trees for his own purposes and then plants and waters an ash to replace them.

Isaiah 44:16b-19 Yes, he warms himself, and says, "Aha, I am warm, I have seen the fire." And the residue of ash he makes a god, even his graven image: he falls down to it, and worships it, and prays to it, and says, "Deliver me; for you are my god." They have not known nor understood: for He has shut their eyes, that they cannot see; and their hearts, that they cannot understand. And none considers in his heart, neither is there knowledge or understanding to say, I have burned part of it in the fire; yes, also I have baked bread upon the coals of it; I have roasted flesh, and eaten it: and shall I make the residue of ash an abomination? shall I fall down to the stock of a tree? He feeds on ashes: a deceived heart has turned him aside, that he cannot deliver his soul, nor say, Is there not a lie in my right hand?

Saddest of all is the person who sits in ashes worshipping the very ashes of the tree provided by the One True God for warmth, cooking bread and meat. When all the blessing is gone by the destructive choices of their own hearts they continue to poke around in the ashes, crying out to the rubble of their life, "You are my god, save me!" An abomination eating ashes, worshipping with a deceived heart and no deliverance for the soul that is holding onto lies. In modern times this is the person who sits using drugs all day (or going to video games, alcohol, pornography, food for pleasure), even when the feeling is no longer a pleasure and it is painful to the body and to the detriment of all other areas of their life-going back to the drug (idol) over and over saying, "You are not giving me that same pleasure, come back, do it again." Eventually God does shut their eyes and they can only be led out of their blindness by another person interceding in prayer on their behalf before God. Otherwise, they are eternally lost in the lies they have believed about their idols.

Isaiah 44:23 Sing, O you heavens; for the Lord has done it: shout, you lower parts of the earth:

break forth into singing, you mountains, O forest, and every tree in it: for the Lord has redeemed Jacob, and glorified himself in Israel.

Let everything on earth praise the Lord for His redemption of Jacob that opened the door for all redemption to take place and for glorifying Himself in Israel so that we can hear of it and know Him more.

Isaiah 55:12-13 For you shall go out with joy, and be led forth with peace: the mountains and the hills shall break forth before you into singing, and all the trees of the field shall clap their hands. Instead of the thorn shall come up the fir tree, and instead of the brier shall come up the myrtle tree: and it shall be to the Lord for a name, for an everlasting sign that shall not be cut off.

Joy, peace, singing praises, even the trees clapping their hands are shown in these verses. Trees of value and beauty blooming in place of thorns and briers. All in worship to the Lord as a sign that we will never be cut off from Him.

Isaiah 56:3 Neither let the son of the stranger, that hath joined himself to the Lord, speak, saying, The Lord hath utterly separated me from his people: neither let the eunuch said, Behold, I am a dry tree.

Whatever our position or relationships, once we have joined to the Lord as believers, do not complain of being called to be different or being a withered dry tree.

Isaiah 57:5 Inflaming yourselves with idols under every green tree, slaying the children in the valleys under the cliffs of the rocks?

Working yourselves into a sexual frenzy before idols under every tree that God has created and even killing your children in worship to idols. It is being in total opposition to God.

Isaiah 60:13 The Glory of Lebanon shall come to you, the fir tree, the pine tree, and the box together, to beautify the place of My sanctuary; and I will make the place of My feet glorious.

Christ in all His Glory will come to all people, both the Israelites and the Gentiles. Every place He enters will become glorious. Use of fir, pine and box trees to beautify His sanctuary.

Isaiah 61:3 To appoint to them that mourn in Zion, to give them beauty for ashes, the oil of joy for mourning, the garment of praise for the spirit of heaviness; that they might be called trees of righteousness, the planting of the Lord, that he might be glorified.

This verse is very familiar to me and to many people. The focus is usually on beauty for ashes. Today's focus is the rest of the verse-The garment of praise for the spirit of heaviness. Oh, how I desire this personally! I want to be called a tree of righteousness, planted by the Lord to glorify Him!

Isaiah 65:22 They shall not build, and another inhabit; they shall not plant, and another eat:

for as the days of a tree are the days of My people, and My select shall long enjoy the work of their hands.

God's chosen people will enjoy the fruits of their labor, the harvest of their fields, the work of their own hands and enjoy it for a long time.

Isaiah 66:17 They that sanctify themselves, and purify themselves in the gardens behind one tree in the midst, eating swine's flesh, and the abomination, and the mouse, shall be consumed together, says the Lord. T

hey hid behind trees in committing abomination against the Lord, being deceived into believing He would not see it. We do not have the power to sanctify ourselves or purify ourselves, if we continue in our sin of self-sufficiency and do not turn to God, we will burn in the fires of hell.

JEREMIAH

Jeremiah 1:11 Moreover the word of the Lord came to me, saying, Jeremiah, what do you see? And I said, I see a rod of an almond tree.

The almond tree is called "the wakeful tree" because it blooms and bears earlier than all the other trees. The prophecy given to Jeremiah is meant to awaken the Israelites to their sins of idol worship and the fact that His anger is burning against them and the punishment is coming.

Jeremiah 2:20 For of old time I have broken your yoke, and burst your bands; and you said, I will not transgress; when upon every high hill and under every green tree you wander, playing the harlot.

A long time ago God freed his people from slavery and sin and brought them into relationship with The One True God, yet the continued to look for another god (cheating on God in idol worship), after promising not to sin anymore, they continued to sin on a large scale under every tree on every mountain.

Jeremiah 3:6 The Lord said to me in the days of Josiah king, "Have you seen the backsliding Israel has done? She is gone up upon every high mountain and under every green tree, and there has played the harlot."

God is asking Jeremiah if he has again observed the Israelites in blatant Idol worship, so soon after promising to return to the Lord.

Jeremiah 3:13 "Only acknowledge your iniquity, that you have transgressed against the Lord your God, and have scattered your (sinful) ways to strangers under every green tree, and you have not obeyed My voice," said the Lord.

Jeremiah is speaking God's plea to confess their sins of idol worship, that they have continued and also brought others into by doing it in public and out in the open. Their blatant disobedience.

Jeremiah 5:17 And they shall eat up your harvest, and your bread, which your sons and daughters should eat: they shall eat up your flocks and herds: they shall eat up your vines and fig trees: they shall impoverish your fenced cities, where you trusted, with the sword.

Placing trust in fences made of wood or stone to protect their cities from enemies, rather than placing their trust in their Powerful God, was a mistake that would cost the Israelites dearly. The fig tree mentioned along with all the other things mentioned were their food supply destroyed by their current enemy bringing on famine and suffering, judgement of the Lord, once again for turning away from Him.

Jeremiah 6:6 For the Lord of hosts has said, "Cut down trees, and cast a mount against Jerusalem: this is the city to be visited; she is totally oppressed in the midst of her."

This verse tells us that the fury of the Lord at the sins of Jerusalem will not be withheld any longer. The Lord himself is instructing the army coming against them to cut down trees for mounting an attack against Jerusalem, leaving only a remnant.

Jeremiah 7:19-20 "Do they provoke me to anger?" says the Lord: "Do they not provoke themselves to the confusion of their own faces?" Therefore, says the Lord God; "Behold, my anger and my fury shall be poured out upon this place, upon man, and upon beast, and upon the trees of the field, and upon the fruit of the ground; and it shall burn, and shall not be quenched."

We are told of God's anger and fury against the sins committed in Jerusalem. Destroying man and beast, both the trees and the fruit on the ground that they produced. His anger shall not be quenched. This judgement is a withdrawal of His original blessing upon Jerusalem.

Jeremiah 8:13 "I will surely consume them," says the Lord: "There shall be no grapes on the vine, nor figs on the fig tree, and the leaf shall fade; and the things that I have given them shall pass from them."

Jeremiah is saying "Judgement of the Lord in the form of consuming them, no grapes, no figs, no leaves. This means loss of food, shade, provision. Every gift from God will be removed from them!"

Jeremiah 10:3-5 For the customs of the people are vain: for as one cuts a tree out of the forest,

the work of the hands of the workman, with the axe. They deck it with silver and with gold;

they fasten it with nails and with hammers that it moves not. They are upright as the palm tree, but speak not: they have to be carried, because they cannot go. Be not afraid of them; for they cannot do evil, neither also is it in them to do good.

These man-made, even dramatically decorated idols are still useless lumps of wood that hold no power, it is all vanity that people think they can create their own gods.

Jeremiah 11:16-19 The Lord called your name, A green olive tree, fair, and of goodly fruit: with the noise of a great tumult he has kindled fire upon it, and the branches of it are broken. For the Lord of hosts, that planted you, has pronounced evil against you, for the evil of the house of Israel and of the house of Judah, which they have done against themselves to provoke me to anger in offering incense unto Baal. And the Lord has given me knowledge of it, and I know it: then He showed me their doings. But I was like a lamb or an ox that is brought to the slaughter; and I knew not that they had devised devices against me, saying, "Let us destroy the tree with the fruit of it, and let us cut him off from the land of the living, that his name may be no more remembered."

The Lord called His people by name, they were young and fair and good, He purified them with fire and broke off the damaged branches (sins). He planted them with all they would need to grow, yet they began and continued in idol worship. God pronounced the evil of their sins, not only idol worship, but a plan to kill Jeremiah (God's prophet) so they no longer had to hear His judgement for their actions. Jeremiah was totally unaware of their plan, until God showed him what they had planned.

JEREMIAH 17:2 While their children remember their altars and their groves by the green trees upon the high hills.

These parents had been instructed to always teach their children God's story in human history, but instead taught them idol worship in groves of trees upon high hills. Did they think that hiding in groves, God could not see what they were doing?

Jeremiah 17:8 For he shall be as a tree planted by the waters, and that spreads out her roots by the river, and shall not see when heat comes, but her leaf shall be green; and shall not be careful in the year of drought, neither shall cease from yielding fruit.

Staying rooted by the waters, getting our nourishment from God and God's word, we can flourish when trials come, keep our strength and youthful energy in all situations and through the years. Even when there is trouble all around us, we will be okay, we will bear fruit in and out of season.

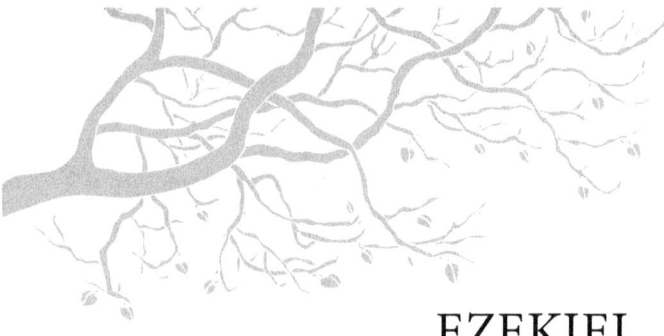

EZEKIEL

Ezekiel 6:13 Then shall you know that I am the Lord, when their slain men shall be among their idols around their altars, upon every high hill, in all the tops of the mountains, and under every green tree, and under every thick oak, the place where they did offer sweet savor to all their idols.

This speaks of death, final judgement to all the idol worshipers, whose bodies will be found lying around the very idols that they placed their trust in. Then all remaining will know for certain that there is only One True God.

Ezekiel 15:1-8 And the word of the Lord came to me, saying, "Son of man, what is the vine tree everything more than any tree, or than a branch which is among the trees of the forest? Shall wood be taken of it to do any work? or will men take a pin of it to hang any vessel on? Behold, it is cast into the fire for fuel; the fire devours both ends of it, and the midst of it is burned. Is it good for any work? Behold, when it was whole, it was good for no work: how much less shall it be good yet for any work, when the fire has devoured it, and it is burned?" Therefore, thus says the Lord God; "As the vine tree among the trees of the forest, which I have given to the fire for fuel, so will I give the inhabitants of Jerusalem. And I will set My face against them; they shall go out from one fire, and another fire shall devour them; and you shall know that I am the Lord, when I set My face against them. And I will make the land desolate, because they have committed a trespass, says the Lord God." Vines served no purpose other than fuel for the fire. You could not build with them or find any other purpose for them. They kindle the fire quickly and burn up totally. Good for nothing before and after the fire.

Ezekiel describes a picture of how useless and sinful the Israelites became even after purification. Just as God gave the vines to burn in the fire, He is now ready to give the sinful Israelites to judgement for their actions. He will no longer be with them, but now be against them in all things. There will be no escape from this judgement. The land will be desolate because of their continued sins without repentance.

Ezekiel 17:1-10 And the word of the Lord came to me, saying, "Son of man, put forth a riddle, and speak a parable to the house of Israel; And say, Thus says the Lord God; A great eagle with great wings, long winged, full of feathers, which had divers colors, came to Lebanon, and took the highest branch of the cedar: He cropped off the top of his young twigs, and carried it into a land of traffic; he set it in a city of merchants. He took also of the seed of the land, and planted it in a fruitful field; he placed it by great waters, and set it as a willow tree. And it grew, and became a spreading vine of low stature, whose branches turned toward him, and the roots of it were under him: so, it became a vine, and brought forth branches, and shot forth sprigs. There was also another great eagle with great wings and many feathers: and, behold, this vine did bend her roots toward him, and shot forth her branches toward him, that he might water it by the furrows of her plantation. It was planted in good soil by great waters, that it might bring forth branches, and that it might bear fruit, that it might be a goodly vine." Say you, "Thus says the Lord God; Shall it prosper? shall He not pull up the roots, and cut off the fruit, that it wither? it shall wither in all the leaves of her spring, even without great power or many people to pluck it up by the roots. Yes, behold, being planted, shall it prosper? shall it not utterly wither, when the east wind touches it? it shall wither in the furrows where it grew?"

Ezekiel shares a riddle or parable-The first great eagle is God and all He did to establish Israel as His people. He reigns supreme, higher than all others. He selected Israel and plucked them out of Egypt and carried them to the promised land, where then had plenty and could be fruitful themselves, gave them cities already established, he supplied all their needs. Israel grew some, but only spreading across the ground not shooting forth towards heaven and God, a vine not a tree. Satan is the second eagle, swooping in with idol worship and empty promises and many turned to him. God had planted them with all they needed to grow in grace and prosper for His kingdom, but they were easily deceived. God can pull this vine up by the roots easily, cut it off from access to Him, so that it withers and dies. Even if Satan replants it, it will never grow properly again.

Ezekiel 17:24 And all the trees of the field shall know that I the Lord have brought down the high tree, have exalted the low tree, have dried up the green tree, and have made the dry tree to flourish: I the Lord have spoken and have done it.

Ezekiel makes a point: All people will know that the Lord has brought leaders low because of their sins. He has flipped the power and authority of the world. The high tree represents religious people who think they no longer need God. The low tree represents the humble, who will be exalted. The green tree thinks it is flourishing on its own terms and in its own power. The dry tree is feeling bereft and in need of a Savior to go on. God knows and sees the truth of each situation.

Ezekiel 20:28 For when I had brought them into the land, for the which I lifted up My hand to give it to them, then they saw every high hill, and all the thick trees, and they offered their sacrifices, and there they presented the provocation of their offerings: there also they made their sweet savor, and poured out there their drink offerings.

The Israelites keep forgetting that God had given them this land from His own hand, went and hid in the thick trees on the high hills to worship idols and false gods in every possible way. Forgetting, also, that God could see them everywhere and always.

Ezekiel 20:45-47 Moreover the word of the Lord came to me, saying, "Son of man, set your face toward the south, and drop your word toward the south, and prophesy against the forest of the south field; And say to the forest of the south, Hear the word of the Lord; Thus says the Lord God; Behold, I will kindle a fire in you, and it shall devour every green tree in you, and every dry tree: the flaming flame shall not be quenched, and all faces from the south to the north shall be burned in it. And all flesh shall see that I the Lord have kindled it: it shall not be quenched."

Ezekiel states: Judgement of the people to the south to the north, fire coming from the Lord to devour them all and nothing can stop it. The judgement will come and destroy everything in its path.

Ezekiel 21:10 It is sharpened to make a sore slaughter; it is decorated that it may glitter: should we then make mirth? it shows contempt for the rod of my son, as every tree.

Speaking of a sword of judgement ready to slaughter, is it funny? Every person that was showing contempt for Christ's convicting to correction and deserving of punishment would be separated from the righteous before the judgement and punishment came.

Ezekiel 27:1-7 The word of the Lord came again unto me, saying, "Now, you son of man, take up a lamentation for Tyrus; And say to Tyrus, O you that is situated at the entry of the sea, which is a merchant of the people for many isles, Thus says the Lord God; O Tyrus, you said, I am of perfect beauty. your borders are in the midst of the seas, your builders have perfected your beauty. They have made all your ship boards of fir trees of Senir: they have taken cedars from Lebanon to make masts for them. Of the oaks of Bashan have they made oars; the company of the Ashurites have made benches of ivory, brought out of the isles of Chittim. Fine linen with embroidered work from Egypt was that which you spread forth to be sails; blue and purple from the isles of Elishah was that which covered them."

A lamentation over the sea city of Tyrus, beginning with a description of the perfect beauty of it and the work of their hands in using fir trees to build ships, with cedar masts, along with some other items for beautifying their ships. A picture in what they thought they could do on their own without any need for God, perfectly self-satisfied. Later in the same lamentation (chapter), God through Ezekiel tells of their total destruction to the point that they will not even be mentioned in history.

Ezekiel 31:1-18 And it came to pass in the eleventh year, in the third month, on the first day of the month, that the word of the Lord came to me, saying, "Son of man, speak to Pharaoh king of Egypt, and to his multitude; Whom are you like in your greatness? Behold, the Assyrian was a cedar in Lebanon with fair branches, and with a shadowing shroud, and of a high stature; and his top was among the thick boughs. The waters made him great, the deep set him up on high with her rivers running around about his plants, and sent out her little rivers unto all the trees of the field. Therefore, his height was exalted above all the trees of the field, and his boughs were multiplied, and his branches became long because of the multitude of waters, when he shot forth. All the fowls of heaven made their nests in his boughs, and under his branches did all the beasts of the field bear their young, and under his shadow dwelt all great nations. Thus, was he fair in his greatness, in the length of his branches: for his root was by great waters. The cedars in the garden of God could not hide him: the fir trees were not like his boughs, and the chestnut trees were not like his branches; nor any tree in the garden of God was like him in his beauty. I have made him fair by the multitude of his branches: so that all the trees of Eden, that were in the garden of God, envied him. Therefore, thus says the Lord God; Because you have lifted up yourself in height, and he has shot up his top among the thick boughs, and his heart is lifted up in his height; I have therefore delivered him into the hands of the mighty one of the heathen; he shall surely deal with him: I have driven him out for his wickedness. And strangers, the terrible of the nations, have cut him off, and have left him: upon the mountains and in all the valleys his branches are fallen, and his boughs are broken by all the rivers of the land; and all the people of the earth are gone down from his shadow, and have left him. Upon his ruin shall all the fowls of the heaven remain, and all the beasts of the field shall be upon his branches: To the end that none of all the trees by the waters exalt themselves for their height, neither shoot up their top among the thick boughs, neither their trees stand up in their height, all that drink water: for they are all delivered to death, to the nether parts of the earth, in the midst of the children of men, with them that go down to the pit." Thus says the Lord God; "In the day when he went down to the grave, I caused a mourning: I covered the deep for him, and I restrained the floods, and the great waters were stayed: and I caused Lebanon to mourn for him, and all the trees of the field fainted for him. I made the nations to shake at the sound of his fall, when I cast him down to hell with them that descend into the pit: and all the trees of Eden, the choice and best of Lebanon, all that drink water, shall be comforted in the nether parts of the earth. They also went down into hell with him unto them that be slain with the sword; and they that were his arm, that dwelt under his shadow in the midst of the heathen. To whom are you like in glory and greatness among the trees of Eden? Yet shall you be brought down with the trees of Eden into the nether parts of the earth: you shalt lie in the midst of the uncircumcised with them that be slain by the sword."

This is Pharaoh and all his multitude, says the Lord God (according to Ezekiel) God's prophet Ezekiel is calling out Pharaoh (his army and all of Egypt) in his pride of being a ruler and thinking he is a god and has any sort of power to do anything on his own. Mocking Pharaoh in asking "You are as great as whom?" He compared him to the Assyrian king, who grew in power and might and ruled a vast part of the known world at that time, including some of the Israelites for a time. The Assyrian king was higher, overshadowing all others and abundantly wealthy in all things. He had plenty to take care of all those who depended on him for his provision. Even the Israelites envied his power, position and wealth. Because of his pride in the work of his own hands and believing he needed nothing or no one else, God's judgement and punishment came. God totally destroyed him: his rule, his kingdom and cast them all into hell for eternity. Even memory of him is no more, all people have left him. God made them all to mourn for him and with him, as they were cast into hell, as well. Again, the question by Ezekiel, "Exactly whom are you like Pharaoh, thinking that you are the glory and greatness of Israel?" You will, also, be brought down and cast into hell with all your multitude. Ezekiel emphasizes that this is a promise from God.

Ezekiel 34:27 And the tree of the field shall yield fruit, and the earth shall yield her increase, and they shall be safe in their land, and shall know that I am the Lord, when I have broken the bands of their yoke, and delivered them out of the hands of those that serve themselves of them.

The Israelites will be freed from bondage to yield fruit and increase. They will be safe again. They will know that I am the Lord by this mighty act of deliverance from slavery to freedom.

Ezekiel 36:30 And I will multiply the fruit of the tree, and the increase of the field, that you shall receive no more reproach of famine among the heathen.

Ezekiel delivers God's promise of abundant blessing for the repentant, returned Israelites. Fellowship with God is restored, no more being starved by slave masters.

Ezekiel 40:16-37 And there were narrow windows to the little chambers, and to their posts within the gate around, and likewise to the arches: and windows were around inward: and upon each post were palm trees. Then brought He me into the outward court, and there were chambers, and a pavement made for the court around: thirty chambers were upon the pavement. And the pavement by the side of the gates over against by the length of the gates was the lower pavement. Then He measured the breadth from the front of the lower gate to the front of the inner court outside, a hundred cubits eastward and northward. And the gate of the outward court that looked toward the north, He measured the length of, and the breadth of. And the little chambers were three on this side and three on that side; and the posts and the arches were after the measure of the first gate: the length was fifty cubits, and the breadth five and twenty cubits. And their windows, and their arches, and their palm trees, were after the measure of the gate that looked toward the east; and they went up to it by seven steps; and the arches were before them. And the gate of the inner court was by the gate toward the north, and toward the east; and he measured from gate to gate a hundred cubits. After that He brought me toward the south, and behold a gate toward the south: and he measured the posts and the arches according to these measures. And there were windows in it and in the arches around, like those windows: the length was fifty cubits, and the breadth five and twenty cubits. And there were seven steps to go up to it, and the arches were before them: and it had palm trees, one on this side, and another on that side, upon the posts. And there was a gate in the inner court toward the south: and He measured from gate to gate toward the south a hundred cubits. And He brought me to the inner court by the south gate: and He measured the south gate according to these measures; And the little chambers, and the posts, and the arches, according to these measures: and there were windows in it and in the arches thereof around: it was fifty cubits long, and five and twenty cubits broad. And the arches around were five and twenty cubits long, and five cubits broad. And the arches were toward the outer court; and palm trees were upon the posts: and the going up to it had eight steps. And He brought me into the inner court toward the east: and He measured the gate according to these measures. And the little chambers, and the posts, and the arches, were according to these measures: and there were windows and, in the arches, around: it was fifty cubits long, and five and twenty cubits broad. And the arches were toward the outward court; and palm trees were upon the posts, on this side, and on that side: and the going up to it had eight steps. And He brought me to the north gate, and measured it according to these measures; The little chambers, the posts, and the arches, and the windows to it around: the length was fifty cubits, and the breadth five and twenty cubits. And the posts were toward the outer court; and palm trees were upon the posts, on this side, and on that side: and the going up to it had eight steps.

There are many chapters in a row that describe an incredibly beautiful, ornate and massive temple used in the worship of the Lord. A guided tour by the Lord himself for Ezekiel. This particular section repeatedly mentions the use of palm trees carved as decoration of the temple. Re-read it and try your best to imagine both the grandeur and the colossal size of it with the Lord as your tour guide.

Ezekiel 41:18-26 And it was made with cherubim and palm trees, so that a palm tree was between a cherub and a cherub; and every cherub had two faces; So that the face of a man was toward the palm tree on the one side, and the face of a young lion toward the palm tree on the other side: it was made through all the house roundabout. From the ground to above the door were cherubim and palm trees made, and on the wall of the temple. The posts of the temple were squared, and the face of the sanctuary; the appearance of the one as the appearance of the other. The altar of wood was three cubits high, and the length thereof two cubits; and the corners thereof, and the length thereof, and the walls thereof, were of wood: and he said unto me, this is the table that is before the Lord. And the temple and the sanctuary had two doors. And the doors had two leaves apiece, two turning leaves; two leaves for the one door, and two leaves for the other door. And there were made on them, on the doors of the temple, cherubim and palm trees, like as were made upon the walls; and there were thick planks upon the face of the porch without. And there were narrow windows and palm trees on the one side and on the other side, on the sides of the porch, and upon the side chambers of the house, and thick planks.

Many trees and types of wood were used in building God's temple in this vision of Ezekiel by very specific instructions. These were followed very obediently to not only build, but also to beautify and worship God in a very specific way, with items and furnishings designed for worship. The most impressive house ever built and specifically for God.

Ezekiel 47:7 Now when I returned, behold, at the bank of the river were very many trees on the one side and on the other.

Continuing in the vision, of a personal tour by the Lord, Ezekiel sees a river with many trees on each side of a river-Signifying the Israelite tribes with some dwelling on either side of the Jordan river.

Ezekiel 47:12 And by the river upon the bank, on this side and on that side, shall grow all trees for food, whose leaf shall not fade, neither shall the fruit be consumed completely: it shall bring forth new fruit according to its months, because their waters they issued out of the sanctuary: and the fruit shall be for food, and the leaf for medicine.

The Lord's guided tour for Ezekiel continues. It seems to be a tour of things in Heaven that reflect like a mirror image of things God created on earth, only much better, even perfected. A tree that is in season at all times providing fruit eternally and leaves for healing eternally because the waters of the river that provide water to the roots flow from the temple of God. What a picture of how we as humans can grow, bloom, heal and produce fruit all through our lives, if (and only if) our own roots reach the waters flowing from God's temple. I am in awe!

DANIEL

Daniel 4:10-26 Thus were the visions of my head in my bed; I saw, and behold a tree in the midst of the earth, and the height of it was great. The tree grew, and was strong, and the height of it reached to heaven, and the sight of it to the end of all the earth: The leaves were fair, and the fruit was much, and in it as food for all: the beasts of the field had shadow under it, and the fowls of the heaven dwelt in the boughs, and all flesh was fed of it. I saw in the visions of my head upon my bed, and, behold, a watcher and a holy one came down from heaven; He cried aloud, and said thus, Cut down the tree, and cut off his branches, shake off his leaves, and scatter his fruit: let the beasts get away from under it, and the fowls from his branches: But, leave the stump of his roots in the earth, even with a band of iron and brass, in the tender grass of the field; and let it be wet with the dew of heaven, and let his portion be with the beasts in the grass of the earth: Let his heart be changed from man's, and let a beast's heart be given to him; and let seven times pass over him. This matter is by the decree of the watchers, and the demand by the word of the holy ones: to the intent that the living may know that the Most High rules in the kingdom of men, and gives it to whoever he will, and sets up over it the basest of men. This dream I, king Nebuchadnezzar, have seen. Now you, O Belteshazzar (Daniel), declare the interpretation of it, because all the wise men of my kingdom are not able to make known to me the interpretation: but you are able; for the spirit of the holy gods is in you.

Then Daniel, whose name was Belteshazzar, was astonished for one hour, and his thoughts troubled him. The king spoke, and said, Belteshazzar, let not the dream, or the interpretation of it, trouble you. Belteshazzar answered and said, my lord, the dream be to them that hate you, and the interpretation of it to your enemies. The tree that you saw, which grew, and was strong, whose height reached unto the heaven, and the sight of it to all the earth; Whose leaves were fair, and the fruit was much, and in it was food for all; under which the beasts of the field dwelt, and upon whose branches the fowls of the heaven had their habitation: It is you, O king, that are grown and become strong: for your greatness is grown, and reaches unto heaven, and your dominion to the end of the earth. And where the king saw a watcher and a holy one coming down from heaven, and saying, Cut the tree down, and destroy it; yet leave the stump of the roots in the earth, even with a band of iron and brass, in the tender grass of the field; and let it be wet with the dew of heaven, and let his portion be with the beasts of the field, till seven times pass over him; This is the interpretation, O king, and this is the decree of the most High, which is come upon my lord the king: That they shall drive you from men, and your dwelling shall be with the beasts of the field, and they shall make you to eat grass as oxen, and they shall wet you with the dew of heaven, and seven times shall pass over you, till you know that the most High rules in the kingdom of men, and gives to whoever he will. And where they commanded to leave the stump of the tree roots; your kingdom shall be returned to you, after that you shall have known that the heavens do rule.

King Nebuchadnezzar has a troubling dream that none of his wise men can interpret. He knows that Daniel (who he renamed Belteshazzar) can interpret the dream because of his connection with the Holy Spirit (whom Nebuchadnezzar mistakenly calls spirit of the holy gods). He misses the entire point of the One True Holy God, but still recognizes that there is something different and special about Daniel. In the dream King Nebuchadnezzar is likened to a tree of great stature, reaching to heaven, seen by all the earth. Everyone had heard of his vast kingdom, power and wealth. Provision by King Nebuchadnezzar of shade and shelter and food. His greatness grew because of this provision for the people. However, God says I will know show you who you are and who has and dispenses power. Nebuchadnezzar will be stripped of all his power and even his sanity by God, He will be cast out to live with the animals for a time. Leaving the root means he can and will be re-established as king after he has time to recognize God and rule with that in mind, for the rest of his days.

HOSEA

Hosea 2:12 And I will destroy her vines and her fig trees, whereof she has said, these are my rewards that my lovers have given me: and I will make them a forest, and the beasts of the field shall eat them.

God will destroy all ill begotten gains. In this particular verse a lady with vineyards and fig orchards gained from lovers (notice the plural) will lose it all because she gained it all in sin. It will be made food for beasts of the field and no longer a blessing to her.

Hosea 9:10 I found Israel like grapes in the wilderness; I saw your fathers as the first ripe in the fig tree at her first time: but they went to Baalpeor, and separated themselves unto that shame;

and their abominations were according as they loved.

Hosea says-God found Israel as ripe as grapes, the first generation ripened for the harvest, but even though they followed Him, they quickly lost sight of Him and turned away to idols (Baal) and loved the idols more than God.

Hosea 14:4-9 I will heal their backsliding; I will love them freely: for my anger is turned away from him. I will be as the dew to Israel: he shall grow as the lily, and spread his roots as Lebanon. His branches shall spread, and his beauty shall be as the olive tree, and his smell as Lebanon. They that dwell under His shadow shall return; they shall revive as the corn, and grow as the vine: the scent of it shall be as the wine of Lebanon. Ephraim shall say, what have I to do any more with idols? I have heard Him, and observed Him: I am like a green fir tree. From God your fruit is found. Who is wise, and he shall understand these things? Prudent, and he shall know them? for the ways of the Lord are right, and the just shall walk in them: but the transgressors shall fall.

Hosea shares that God is willing to heal the backsliding Israelites. He loves them freely, regardless of their sins; He chooses to not be angry with them any longer. He will refresh them as the dew refreshes the earth. And the Israelites will grow in beauty and spread. The olive tree that is Israel will be providing the story of God to the rest of the world, and send forth a sweet aroma. All who hear and receive this story will return to the shade and protection of God to be revived and grow in grace. All having a sweet aroma. Ephraim will turn away from their idol worship because they heard and observed God. They will again stand strong like a green fir tree (evergreen). As long as we continue to turn to God to be fed (the Word), we can become wise in understanding the ways of God and be prudent and best of all be known by God. His ways are always right, if we are just, we will walk in them, but unrepentant sinners will fall.

JOEL

Joel 1:7 He has laid my vine waste, and barked my fig tree: He has made it clean bare, and cast it away; the branches of it are made white.

Joel makes this point that God destroyed the crooked and twisted vine that was growing, and He stripped the tree of is bark, making it clean bare. He cast away the vine and the bark, even cleaning every branch bare. Stripping us of our sins and humbling us, leaving us feeling bare before Him with nowhere to hide, but we are made new with all our sins cast away from us.

Joel 1:11-12 Be ashamed, O you men; howl, O you vinedressers, for the wheat and barley; because the harvest of the field is perished. The vine is dried up, and the fig tree languished; the pomegranate tree, the palm tree also, and the apple tree, even all the trees of the field, are withered: because joy is withered away from the sons of men.

We should all be ashamed and howling because we have been called as vinedressers to help others see their sins and need for the Real Vinedresser in their lives, but we go on and allow them to perish, even though they are ripe for the harvest, all dried up and languishing every sort and type withered. All because we forgot our own joy in the Lord, that we should be sharing with others.

Joel 1:19 O Lord, to You will I cry: for the fire has devoured the pastures of the wilderness, and the flame has burned all the trees of the field.

People crying out to God because fire has destroyed pastures to feed their livestock and trees. Both of these are food sources and the people are fearing hunger or famine. They forget that God can provide even in this situation. Crying out for help from God is the best place to start and perhaps even the purpose of this destruction-to get them to refocus on God.

Joel 2:21-27 Fear not, O land; be glad and rejoice: for the Lord will do great things.

Be not afraid, you beasts of the field: for the pastures of the wilderness do spring,

for the tree bears her fruit, the fig tree and the vine do become strong. Be glad then, you children of Zion, and rejoice in the Lord your God: for He has given you the former rain moderately, and He will cause to come down for you the rain, the former rain, and the latter rain in the first month. And the floors shall be full of wheat, and the fats shall overflow with wine and oil. And I will restore to you the years that the locust has eaten, the cankerworm, and the caterpillar, and the palmerworm, my great army which I sent among you. And you shall eat in plenty, and be satisfied, and praise the name of the Lord your God, that has dealt wondrously with you: and my people shall never be ashamed. And you shall know that I am in the midst of Israel, and that I am the Lord your God, and none else: and My people shall never be ashamed.

Here is a continuation of the last section that was conviction of the Israelites sins. Joel sharing the message "Now fear not Israel, be glad and rejoice for the Lord has chosen to do great things (once again to restore you). Do not be afraid that you will continue in your sins. Because you will again spring forth in growth and bear fruit for the Kingdom of God. Your strength will return. God provided your needs moderately before, but shall now provide them very abundantly. Your harvest (of souls) shall be so great, it will be overflowing. God can erase the years that Satan has held you trapped and even the retribution that God sent among you, to bring you back to Him. You will once again be abundantly blessed, satisfied and praise the name of the Lord Your God and no more idol worship. God has dealt wondrously with us and we will never be put to shame again! We will know for sure that He is God and there is no other like Him. No more shame, because He cast away our sins and forgiven and restored us to Him!"

AMOS

Amos 4:9 I have smitten you with blasting and mildew: when your gardens and your vineyards and your fig trees and your olive trees increased, the palmerworm devoured them: yet have you not returned unto Me, says the Lord.

Amos says "The Lord sent destruction of the food supply in the forms of blasting (wind, probably tornado or hurricane strength), mildew and the palmerworm to destroy figs, olive trees and vineyards to get the attention of the Israelites. Yet, they still chose not to return to Him."

ZECHARIAH

Zechariah 1:8-11 I saw by night, and behold a man riding on a red horse, and he stood among the myrtle trees that were in the bottom; and behind him were there red horses, speckled, and white. Then said I, "O my lord, what are these?" And the angel that talked with me said to me, "I will show you what these are." And the man that stood among the myrtle trees answered and said, "These are they whom the Lord hath sent to walk to and fro through the earth." And they answered the angel of the Lord that stood among the myrtle trees, and said, "We have walked to and fro through the earth, and, behold, all the earth sits still, and is at rest."

A vision of Zechariah. He saw among the myrtle trees a man on a red horse leading other horses (notice it does not mention other riders). Upon asking about them, the angel guide of Zechariah agrees to show him what they are and the man on the red horse says these are the ones the Lord appointed to go over all the earth and observe people (the horses). The horses speak, responding that they have done as instructed and all is at rest (it is night, as mentioned earlier in the verse). We have seen a donkey speak earlier to Balaam, and now horses both on watch for God as appointed and speaking to report back their findings. Oh, how exciting!"

Zechariah 4:3 And two olive trees by it, one on the right side of the bowl, and the other on the left side.

These are explained in the next verse.

Zechariah 4:11-14 Then answered I, and said unto him, "What are these two olive trees on the right side of the candlestick and on the left side?' And I answered again, and said to him, "What are these two olive branches which through the two golden pipes empty the golden oil out of themselves?" And he answered me and said, "Do you not know what these are?" And I said, "No, my lord." Then he said, "These are the two anointed ones, that stand by the Lord of the whole earth."

The two olive trees are the two anointed ones that stand beside the Lord- What a place of honor! They are standing and emptying the golden oil out of themselves through two golden pipes, which represents pouring themselves out to tell others about their Lord!

Zechariah 3:9b-10 And I will remove the iniquity of that land in one day. In that day, says the Lord of hosts, shall you call every man his neighbor under the vine and under the fig tree.

Zechariah wants us to know that God has the power to turn things around completely in one day, removing our sins from us and restoring us to be in community with others in the shade of his protection and provision.

Zechariah 11:2 Open your doors, O Lebanon, that the fire may devour your cedars. Howl, fir tree; for the cedar is fallen; because the mighty are spoiled: howl, O, you oaks of Bashan; for the forest of the vintage is come down.

A warning-get ready for the judgement of your sins, fire is coming to destroy, utterly. Cry out in pain, sinners will be felled like mighty trees. God has come down for judgement and punishment. (According to Zechariah)

MATTHEW

Matthew 3:10 And now the axe is laid to the root of the trees: then every tree which bring no good fruit is cut down, and cast into the fire.

The time to pay for the choices made in life, if we continue in sin and make no difference for the glory and kingdom of God, we will be cast into the fires of hell.

Matthew 7:17-20 Even so every good tree brings forth good fruit; but a corrupt tree brings forth evil fruit. A good tree cannot bring forth evil fruit, neither can a corrupt tree brings forth good fruit. Every tree that brings not forth good fruit is cut down, and cast into the fire. Wherefore by their fruits you shall know them.

Living and walking in God's will and following His plan we will produce good fruit (love, joy, peace, patience, kindness, gentleness, goodness, faithfulness, self-control), if we do this, we cannot produce evil fruit (hate, sadness, anger, impatience, selfishness, rudeness, meanness and no control over our actions). Everyone who chooses not to follow God will be cast into hell fire. True believers will be known by their fruits of love, joy, peace, patience, kindness, gentleness, goodness, faithfulness, self-control,

Matthew 12:33 Either make the tree good, and his fruit good; or else make the tree corrupt, and his fruit corrupt: for the tree is known by his fruit.

We choose in our daily lives and actions to be good or corrupt. We need to stop swaying back and forth in the breeze and fully commit to God.

Matthew 13:32 Which indeed is the least of all seeds: but when it is grown, it is the greatest among herbs, and becometh a tree, so that the birds of the air come and lodge in the branches thereof.

As tiny as a mustard seed- even when we feel so small and insignificant in the larger scale of things, God is able to use us and grow us into something amazing that provides safety and shelter for those damaged by the sinful world.

Matthew 21:8-9 And a very great multitude spread their garments in the way; others cut down branches from the trees, and strew them in the way. And the multitudes that went before, and that followed, cried, saying, Hosanna to the Son of David: Blessed is he that comes in the name of the Lord; Hosanna in the highest.

On His way into Jerusalem, the crowds are praising the Lord with tree branches by decorating the road He will travel on His journey to the cross and glorification in rising again, with victory over death and hell. Hosanna in the highest!

Matthew 21:19-21 And when He saw a fig tree on the way, he came to it, and found nothing there, but leaves only, and said to it, "Let no fruit grow on you here forward forever." And presently the fig tree withered away. And when the disciples saw it, they marveled, saying, "How soon is the fig tree withered away!" Jesus answered and said to them, "Verily I say to you, If you have faith, and doubt not, you shall not only do this which is done to the fig tree, but also if you shall say unto this mountain, Be you removed, and be you cast into the sea; it shall be done. And all things, whatever you shall ask in prayer, believing, you shall receive."

I understand Matthew to be saying, that Jesus hungry found a fig tree with leaves that was bearing no fruit and cursed it forevermore. Just as we will be cursed if we bear no fruit. Immediately it withered and the disciples were amazed that he had this power over nature. Jesus again points out that they are still lacking in faith or they would know that they could do this same thing and so much more in His powerful name. Prayer and believing faith are the keys to receiving.

Matthew 24:32 Now learn a parable of the fig tree; When his branch is yet tender, and puts forth leaves, you know that summer is nigh, Matthew sharing this story, Jesus speaks often of fig trees.

In this verse the state of the tree is an indication of what is coming soon. This is in the middle of a passage speaking of end times.

MARK

Mark 8:23-25 And He took the blind man by the hand, and led him out of the town; and when He had spit on his eyes, and put His hands upon him, He asked him if he saw anything. And he looked up, and said, I see men as trees walking. After that He put his hands again upon his eyes, and made him look up: and he was restored, and saw every man clearly.

The significance of the blind man first seeing men walking around as trees could be only that his vision was not completely clear. However, Christ had both the knowledge and ability to heal him completely on the first try, so I am sure there is more significance in this part of the story. Perhaps it points to the story of the prophet seeing men walking around as living trees and dead trees.

Mark 11:11b-14 He went out to Bethany with the twelve. And on the morrow, when they were come from Bethany, He was hungry: And seeing a fig tree afar off having leaves, He came, if happily He might find anything on it: and when He came to it, he found nothing but leaves; for the time of figs was not yet. And Jesus answered and said to it, no man eat fruit of you hereafter forever. And his disciples heard it.

This story is repeated from Matthew 24:32 from Mark's perspective.

LUKE

Luke 3:9 And now the axe is laid to the root of the trees: every tree that brings forth no good fruit is cut down, and cast into the fire.

A story repeated from Matthew 3:10 from Luke's perspective.

Luke 6:43-45 For a good tree does not bring forth corrupt fruit; neither does a corrupt tree bring forth good fruit. For every tree is known by his own fruit. For of thorns men do not gather figs, nor of a bramble bush gather they grapes. A good man out of the good treasure of his heart brings forth that which is good; and an evil man out of the evil treasure of his heart brings forth that which is evil: for of the abundance of the heart his mouth speaks.

Matthew 7:17-20 retold from Luke's perspective. Luke adds clarification that whatever is truly in our hearts will be reflected in our actions and our speech.

Luke 13:6-9 He spoke this parable too; "A certain man had a fig tree planted in his vineyard; and he came and sought fruit on it, and found none. Then said he to the dresser of his vineyard, Behold, these three years I come seeking fruit on this fig tree, and find none: cut it down; why bother the ground with it? And he answering said unto him, Lord, let it alone this year also, till I shall dig about it, and dung it: And if it bears fruit, well: and if not, then after that you shall cut it down."

Another parable about a fig tree. The fig tree represents a person. His vineyard represents God's Kingdom, fruit represents the righteousness (or lack of it) in the person. The vinedresser is Christ. Three years is the period of time the person was called to right living, yet, choosing to continue in their sin. This sentence, "cut it down, why bother with the ground anymore?" seems to show God as angry at their sins. Christ then appears to intercede on behalf of the person. Let us cultivate them for one more year and then if they still turn away, after this final chance, then cut them down.

Luke 13:18-19 Then said He, what is the kingdom of God like? And what does it resemble? It is like a grain of mustard seed, which a man took, and cast into his garden; and it grew, and waxed a great tree; and the fowls of the air lodged in the branches of it.

According to Luke, the kingdom of God is like the tiniest of seeds that grows into the largest of trees, it provides: shade, shelter, food, fuel for fires to warm us and for cooking, wood for building, and so much more. The faith planted in me was very small at the beginning and has changed me more than I can explain and changed the trajectory of my family forevermore. The beginning of Christianity was Christ and His twelve disciples that changed the world forevermore.

Luke 17:6 And the Lord said, if you had faith as a grain of mustard seed, you might say unto this sycamore tree, be plucked up by the roots, and be planted in the sea; and it should obey you.

Even a tiny amount of faith in God's power can do great and amazing things. If is the tiniest word with the greatest power in this verse. We each face our "if" every day.

Luke 19:1-10 And Jesus entered and passed through Jericho. And, behold, there was a man named Zacchaeus, which was the chief among the publicans, and he was rich. And he sought to see Jesus who he was; and could not for the press, because he was little of stature. And he ran before, and climbed up into a sycamore tree to see him: for he was to pass that way. And when Jesus came to the place, he looked up, and saw him, and said unto him, "Zacchaeus, hurry, and come down; for today I must abide at your house." And he hurried, and came down, and received him joyfully. And when they saw it, they all murmured, saying, that He was gone to be guest with a man that is a sinner. And Zacchaeus stood, and said to the Lord; "Behold, Lord, half of my goods I give to the poor; and if I have taken anything from any man by false accusation, I restore him fourfold." And Jesus said to him, "This day is

Salvation come to this house, for as he also is a son of Abraham. For the Son of Man is come to seek and to save that which was lost."

A most beloved story taught to children in Sunday school, but I fear some of the main points are missed. Zacchaeus was a rich, but short man (who became wealthy by cheating people, as a tax collector). This sinful man was so moved by hearing of Jesus that he just had to see Him. Because of the crowd and his being short, he climbed up a tree just to catch a glimpse of Jesus, along the route He was to take. When Jesus came and looked up and saw Him, He was impressed to see the effort the little man put in to seeing Him and called Him down, saying I am going to your house today. Zacchaeus was excited to hear this and hurried down and joyfully received Jesus into his home and his heart. Others watching were jealous and said out loud, why would Jesus choose that sinner over us, we are so much more Holy than Zacchaeus. This up close and personal meeting with Jesus immediately changed Zacchaeus to want to be a righteous man. It moved his heart and soul, changing him forevermore. He vowed on the spot to give half of what he owned to the poor and repay anyone he had cheated times four. Luke tells us that Jesus responds with, "Today you and your household have been saved, for you are also a son of Abraham. For the Son of Man is come to seek and to save that which was lost. The awesome part of this is the "is". It doesn't say has, but is, present tense. Jesus **is** come to seek and to save that which was lost. He is still seeking and saving the lost today. Amazing.

Luke 21:28-30 And when these things begin to come to pass, then look up, and lift up your heads; for your redemption draws near. And he spoke to them a parable; Behold the fig tree, and all the trees; When they now shoot forth, you see and know of your own selves that summer is now near at hand.

A repeated prophecy of what to watch for as the end times draw nearer.

Luke 23:31 For if they do these things in a green tree, what shall be done in the dry?

If Christians sin out in the open, what shall sinners do in the depth of their sin and in darkness.

JOHN

John 1:47-51 Jesus saw Nathanael coming to Him, and said of him, "Behold an Israelite indeed, in whom is no deceit?" Nathanael said to Him, "How do You know me?" Jesus answered and said to him, "Before Philip called you, when you were under the fig tree, I saw you." Nathanael answered and said to Him, "Rabbi, You are the Son of God; You are the King of Israel." Jesus answered and said unto him, "Because I said to you, I saw you under the fig tree, you believed? You shall see greater things than these. And he said to him, "Verily, verily, I say to you, later you shall see heaven open, and the angels of God ascending and descending upon the Son of Man."

Nathanael was brought to Jesus by Phillip, after he had just said, "Nothing good comes out of Nazareth", while standing under a fig tree. Upon meeting Jesus,

Nathanael immediately believed because Jesus knew him inside and out and had seen him under the fig tree before he came with Phillip to meet him. The subtlety of the story is that Jesus saw him and heard how he had insulted Him about being from Nazareth, before he ever met him. Notice the question mark at the end of Jesus statement about Nathanael, "Behold an Israelite indeed, in whom there is no deceit?" Not a statement, so much as a question, "Is this really possible to be an Israelite without deceit?' Jesus also appears to be letting him know that this was not much bases for belief, just the fact that He knew him and that Nathanael would see much greater things later, "Angels going up and down from Heaven upon the Son of Man (Jesus)"

John 12:12-13 On the next day, many people that came to the feast, when they heard that Jesus was coming to Jerusalem, took branches of palm trees, and went forth to meet him, and cried, Hosanna: Blessed is the King of Israel that comes in the name of the Lord.

Branches of the very trees that He created used in the worship of Christ on His final return to Jerusalem. For a brief moment in time some Israelites got it right.

ACTS

Acts 5:29-30 Then Peter and the other apostles answered and said, we ought to obey God rather than men. The God of our fathers raised up Jesus, whom you killed and hung on a tree.

Peter is pointing out that we should obey God and not men. Because men (the religious leaders of that day) were fully responsible for this. It is the other end of the ultimate twisting of what God provided for our blessing. Religious leaders in their pride and sin killed Jesus and hung Him on a tree. He was willing to face this humiliation and death for my sins and yours. The Creator of both the human and the tree. rejected and hung on the tree by the ones that He had created to love, honor and glorify Him.

Acts 10:39-43 How God anointed Jesus of Nazareth with the Holy Ghost and with power: who went about doing good, and healing all that were oppressed of the devil; for God was with Him. And we are witnesses of all things which he did, both in the land of the Jews, and in Jerusalem; whom they killed and hanged on a tree: Him God raised up the third day, and showed him openly; Not to all the people, but unto witnesses chosen previously by God, even to us, who did eat and drink with Him after he rose from the dead. And he commanded us to preach to the people, and to testify that it is He which was ordained of God to be the Judge of quick and dead. To Him give all the prophets witness, that through His name whosoever believes in him shall

receive remission of sins.

Even though Jesus was given power and the Holy Spirit, and anointed by God, even though He only did good everywhere He went, even though He healed and cast out demons, and God was with him. We (the disciples and many other witnesses) saw it all happen throughout the land of the Jews and right here in Jerusalem. You killed Him and hung Him on a tree. But that is not the end of the story, for God raised Him up on the third day and showed Him openly to believers that God had chosen previously and to the disciples. We ate and drank with Jesus. He commanded us to preach that He was ordained by God to Judge all people dead and alive. Also, to preach that he is the fulfillment of all the prophecies of the Old Testament. And the best news of all time, **"That whoever believes in Him shall receive remission (the cancellation of debt, charge, or penalty) of their sins."**

Acts 13:29-30 And when they had fulfilled all that was written of Him, they took him down from the tree, and laid him in a sepulcher. But God raised him from the dead:

After fulfilling all the prophecies from the Old Testament regarding Jesus that had been written. They removed His dead body from the tree that it was hanging on and placed Him in a tomb. But, Hallelujah, God raised Him from the dead.

ROMANS

Romans 11:16-24 For if the first fruit is holy, the lump is also holy: and if the root is holy, so are the branches. And if some of the branches be broken off, and you, being a wild olive tree, were grafted in among them, and with them partakes of the root and fatness of the olive tree; Boast not against the branches. But if you boast, you bear not the root, but the root bears you.

According to the Apostle Paul, Jesus is the first fruit and thus Holy, we are the lump and Holy because we know Him. Jesus is the root and we are the branches. We can remain Holy if we remain connected to the root. Gentiles are the wild olive tree, broken off from connection to Jesus, but we can be grafted back in and enjoy the same relationship as the Israelites. The Israelites should not be puffed up with pride against the Gentiles. If they do think they are better, then they are no longer connected to Jesus, but lost in selfishness, again.

JAMES

James 3:12 Can the fig tree, my brethren, bear olive berries? either a vine, figs? so can no fountain both yield salt water and fresh.

We are who God says we are and doing what God designed up to do. We cannot do, be or produce anything other than what God plans for us- successfully. If we try, over time God will bring us back to His plan and design.

1 PETER

1 Peter 2:24 Who His own self bore our sins in His own body on the tree, that we, being dead to sins, should live to righteousness: by whose stripes you were healed.

The heart of the Bible is that Jesus chose to bear our sins in His own body, hanging on that tree, so that we being dead in our sins, might rise to new life in Him, so we could live righteously and be healed by the stripes He received in our place. Thank you, God, for your plan of Salvation.

JUDE

Jude 1:12 These are spots in your feasts of charity, when they feast with you, feeding themselves without fear: clouds they are without water, carried about of winds; trees whose fruit withers, without fruit, twice dead, plucked up by the roots;

People attending church and enjoying the feast of God's Word and the blessing, proudly feeding themselves. Clouds without water, blown about by the wind-They are dry and brittle, when someone catches on to their act they blow up and go to a different church. Any fruit they plant withers and dies-because God is not in it. Twice dead-natural and physical death. Plucked up by the roots-cast into hell at the end.

REVELATION

Revelation 2:7 He that has an ear, let him hear what the Spirit said unto the churches; To him that overcomes will I give to eat of the tree of life, which is in the midst of the paradise of God.

This verse seems to shout, Listen, all who have ears to what the Holy Spirit says to the churches: Most incredible, the Alpha and Omega, the beginning and the end, return to the paradise God designed like the Garden of Eden with free and eternal access to the Tree of Life again for all believers, evermore!

Revelation 6:13 And the stars of heaven fell unto the earth, even as a fig tree casts her untimely figs, when she is shaken of a mighty wind. The stars fell to the earth without warning like a fig tree that drops all of its fruit, not yet ripened, unexpectedly when a mighty wind blows.

The end of the first beginning and a fresh new start for believers.

Revelation 7:1 And after these things I saw four angels standing on the four corners of the earth, holding the four winds of the earth, that the wind should not blow on the earth, nor on the sea, nor on any tree.

Angels holding back the winds at the end of times.

Revelation 7:3 Saying, hurt not the earth, neither the sea, not the trees, till we have sealed the servants of God on their foreheads.

God's blessing will continue upon the earth until His chosen ones are sealed. Mentions trees specifically along with earth and sea-placing a very high value on trees.

Revelation 8:7 The first angel sounded, and there followed hail and fire mingled with blood, and they were cast upon the earth: and the third part of trees was burnt up, and all green grass was burnt up. One third of the trees burned up and all the grasses burned up leaves the earth somewhat barren.

Removing the blessing of God in judgement and vastly reducing the amount of food available.

Revelation 11:4 These are the two olive trees, and the two candlesticks standing before the God of the earth.

These two olive trees are the two anointed ones that stand by the Lord of the whole earth, mentioned in the vision of **Zechariah (Chapter 4).**

Revelation 22:2 In the midst of the street of it, and on either side of the river, was there the tree of life, which bare twelve manners of fruit, and yielded her fruit every month: and the leaves of the tree were for the healing of the nations.

How majestic, the tree of life growing on both sides of the river in heaven, bearing 12 kinds of fruit on the tree, bearing fruit in and out of season, all 12 months, the leaves bring healing to the nations. I believe this is the same tree that was available to Adam and Eve in the Garden of Eden before sin and the fall.

Revelation 22:14 Blessed are they that do his commandments, that they may have right to the tree of life, and may enter in through the gates into the city.

The reward for following His commandments is the blessing of the right to eternal access to the tree of life and admission to heaven through the city gates. The beginning and The END (which takes us back to His original plan).

SUMMARY

Words to sum all of this up are overwhelming to me.

Simply Trees by God's Design states that the trees are simple, however their function and purpose in the lives of humans is very complex, indeed.

Trees provide oxygen to breath, fruit to eat, wood for both fuel and building, aromatic wood for offerings. This informs us about God's love for us.

The fact that they produce fruit with seeds that reproduce more trees points to God's plan that humans exist on the earth for as long as He desires it.

They were planned in all their design and intricate detail by God before humans were created, to be an additional provision for us. This points to God's absolute wisdom.

Evergreen trees bring to mind a picture of our promise of eternal life!

Researching the sizes, shapes and variety of trees could fill volumes. Some are purely here for their beauty and our enjoyment. This points to God's artistic creativity and expansive knowledge.

Watching the seasons of trees can give us a visual of our own spiritual renewal. This points to lessons to be learned about our own walk with God.

Anyone, anywhere can look around and see trees or something made of wood. So many of us have homes made of wood, furniture made of wood and some even have beautiful carved wood decorations in our homes. This shows that we put our trust in the provision of God to supply all our needs.

Trees in parables teach us about God and His plan for eternity.

Trees reaching to heaven and God show the posture of praise we should all have.

Trees singing and praising at Christ's return to judge the earth, it just blows my mind to envision this.

Access to the tree of life in heaven shows God's love for eternity for all who choose to follow Him.

Reflections

THE AZALEA AND THE SNAIL

I was walking along on a trail and thinking about my growth as a Christian. I look back and see places where my outlook was wrong and then I came to the knowledge that it was wrong and I changed my attitude and actions. I thought, "How would I have believed that lie?"

As I was walking, I saw this beautiful, abundant azalea bush. I walked past it and then went back to snap a picture. It was so covered with blossoms that some had shed off to the ground. I just took in the beauty and thought about bearing abundant fruit as a Christian. On the next pass by this beautiful, pink bush, I noticed that some of the blooms that had fallen to the ground had withered and died and I thought of the story of the sower and the seeds-How some who believed did not remain in the faith, but withered away.

On my next lap, I noticed a snail with a big shell on its back making its way ever so slowly across the trail. Again, I walked right past it and turned back to snap a picture. I thought of my own life journey and burdens that I have carried that were too heavy for me. Just as this snail's shell seemed disproportionate to its tiny body, my own burdens were too heavy to bear alone. I thought of my own snail's pace journey, moving ever so slowly, inch by inch, to the next level of freedom in Christ.

I recalled mistakes I had made along the way, wrong attitudes and actions, based on the information I had at that point in my history. I wondered, "How could I have been so dumb?'

This morning, in my study, I came across the answer to all my pondering. I am only held accountable for the truth that I know at this point of my journey. It revealed the following on my prayer walk.

Just as those azalea blooms unfolded in the sunlight and shed in their glorious abundance and then wither on the ground-My old faulty beliefs wither as they are replaced with true wisdom.

Don't beat yourself up over past mistakes, made when you didn't know better. Be gracious with yourself and receive the mercy offered to you. Offer gratitude for the new level of growth and wisdom that has been revealed to you by Christ, joyfully and with perseverance!

As for me, I will continue my snail's pace journey with endurance to the final joy of seeing Christ-face to face!

INTENTION

Thoughts and direction of the heart
God knows exactly where we start.

Our intention to help, never to harm
Fans the flame, keeping others warm.

Intention to love, intention for good
Intention to give, just as we should.

Sometimes our intention can be swayed,
By hurt and pain that others have made.

Our hearts can become bitter and cruel
No longer seeking or using God's tools.

We can be blinded or caught up in pain
Until we no longer see the Lamb that was slain.

Our intention and posture must always return
To Christ, once our own lesson, we learn.

Repentance and grace, our gift to receive
As quickly as we repent and believe.

Keeping our intentions divine and pure
Will lead to a walk that is strong and sure.

Intention to share God's gift of love
Brings blessed abundance from above.

Extending the same acceptance and grace
As we strive to keep seeking His Face.

THE DISCIPLE WHOM JESUS LOVED

The book of John

This term "the disciple whom Jesus loved" does not state "the disciple whom Jesus loved most", but simply "the disciple whom Jesus loved". Quite clearly, He loved them all dearly. Just as He loves all of His followers dearly.

Written in the book of John, by John-himself.

i. Because he was certain that he was loved by Jesus

ii. Because his entire identity was wrapped up in the knowledge of this love

iii. Because rather than drawing attention to himself, he wanted all things to point to Jesus Christ, including his own name.

iv. This is humbly stated, "the disciple whom Jesus loved" as in John saying, I do not matter, who I am does not matter, "All that matters is who I am in Christ, dwelling in the midst of His love for me!"

John 19:26-27 When Jesus therefore saw His mother, and the disciple standing by, whom He loved, He saith unto his mother, Woman, behold thy son! Then saith He to the disciple, Behold thy mother! And from that hour that disciple took her unto his own home.

Not only loved by Jesus, but trusted with the ongoing care of His mother Mary after Jesus was gone from earth.

John 20:2-10 Then she ran and cometh to Simon Peter, and the other disciple whom Jesus loved, and saith unto them, "They have taken away the Lord out of the sepulcher, and we know not where they have laid him." Peter therefore went forth, and that other disciple, and came to the sepulcher. So, they ran both together: and the other disciple did outrun Peter, and came first to the sepulcher. And he stooping down, and looking in, saw the linen clothes lying; yet went he not in. Then cometh Simon Peter following him, and went into the sepulcher, and seeing the linen clothes lie, and the napkin, that was about his head, not lying with the linen clothes, but wrapped together in a place by itself. Then went in also the other disciple, which came first to the sepulcher, and he saw, and believed. For as yet they knew not the scripture, that he must rise again from the dead. Then the disciples went away again unto their own home.

Not only loved by Jesus, but loving Jesus in return and hoping and eager, displayed in his outrunning Peter to the tomb, to find out what was going on.

John 21:7 Therefore that disciple whom Jesus loved saith unto Peter, it is the Lord.

Not only loved by Jesus, but recognizing Him from afar.

John 21:20 Then Peter, turning about, seeing the disciple whom Jesus loved following; which also leaned on his breast at supper, and said, Lord, which is he that will betray thee?

Not only loved by Jesus, but leaning in close to His heart in complete submission and attentiveness.

1. How are you responding to being loved by Jesus?
2. Does your identity in Christ identify you, when others are asked about you?
3. How attentive and submissive are you to Jesus calling in your life?

More of you Lord, less of me, is my desire, that others see!

UNDULATIONS OF LIFE

As we make our way through each day, our lives ever ebbing and flowing.

Even when things seem still and quiet on the surface, there is much movement beneath.

There are peaks in which we experience vibrations of joy…finding love, wedding days, holding your newborn child for the first time.

In these joyful times, we are so full that we are overflowing with love and gratitude.

Then we experience the valleys, that seem unending and insurmountable…loss of a loved one, pain inflicted by those we trust most or disease in our own bodies.

In these difficult times, we are at a loss only seeking comfort and calm.

On this journey called life, the only real constant is its undulating change, within our bodies and in the world around us.

As long as God grants us the breath of life in our bodies, there is always hope. There may be the smallest fluttering of hope, and we grasp it like a drowning man. It can build and grow to a pulsating feeling that given time, everything will be okay, or even good.

Looking back across your own life, I am sure you can see the movement, the ebb and flow, the rising and falling, the crashing and the breaking of the waves. The breaking is often needed to destroy something that we would not otherwise let go of.

Looking ahead, from wherever you stand right now…feel the gravity of the waves moving you ever forward. Take comfort in the undulations reminding you that change is always on its way.

The undeniable joy when we are riding the crest of the wave, may seem endless in that moment.

Yet, from the highest peaks, we fall. So many without a cord of hope holding them secure.

When the waves are crashing against the rocks, seemingly destroying life as we know it. Some do not know where to turn for hope, to go forward.

Each of us who know this hope should want to share it, to praise and be excited when others are on the mountaintop and to be their comfort when life is falling apart.

Psalm 89:9 You (God) rule the raging sea, when its waves rise, You still them.

Lord,

Lead us each to be present in Your presence enough that we can extend the hope that You fill us with to others. Let us be aware of the needs of those around us and use us to meet those needs.

Amen

HOW GOD SEES YOU…

God sees you as wonderfully made
Worthy in His eyes

God sees you as intimately acquainted
Loved, ignore the lies

God sees how wonderful are your ways
Capable of great things

God sees you as precious in his sight
Desirable, what joy this brings

God sees you as known and still loved
Forgiven and free

God knows your thoughts as precious to Him
How can this be?

God makes your days filled with true
Significance in Him

God wove you in your mother's womb
Not by any whim

God does not make mistakes
Can you now see?

God saved you by His grace
To live eternally!

JEREMIAH 29: 11-14

Jeremiah 29:11 For I know the plans I have for you, declares the Lord, plans for your welfare and not for evil, to give you a future and a hope!

This verse is an anthem for many of us! We speak it as a promise from the Lord, which it is. I have it on a plate that I hand painted in my china cabinet. It gives me hope, when things aren't going my way. So many of us have this one memorized and it gives us hope, which is excellent. However, we fail to read or learn the verses that follow it. These verses hold power and purpose-beyond hope!

Jeremiah 29:12 Then you will call upon Me and come to Me and pray to ME and I will hear you.

First, in verse 11 we become aware that He has a good plan for our lives. Next, we call upon Him to complete it. We draw near to His loving presence. We pray to Him for guidance...And He will hear us!

Jeremiah 29:13 You will seek Me and find Me, when you seek Me with all your heart.

He says it again to make sure we got it. Seek Me and find Me. How? With all your heart seek Me. A pivotal word here is when. That is our decision and action and timeline-When. When, we make it a priority in our busy lives to seek God and pray. When we order everything in our lives around God's loving presence. When, we draw near in prayer. Then, we will find Him, our God of pure love, our faithful friend, our strength in the storm. Jeremiah 29:11 is a promise followed by a command of obedience in the following verses.

Jeremiah 29:14 I will be found by you, declares the Lord and I will restore your fortunes and gather you from all the nations and all the places where I have driven you, declares the Lord and I will bring you back to the place from which I sent you into exile. And it ends with another promise, when you return to me, I will restore all that you have lost and will gather you back into my loving presence, from the place I exiled you, in your sin. Three times the Lord declares promises in these verses. A declaration is a powerful way of speaking a promise. Declaration means a " a formal or explicit statement or announcement" or "the formal announcement of the beginning of a state or condition".

The Lord is giving us a formal and explicit promise that announces the beginning of our state of being when we draw nearer to His loving presence! How awesome is that?

THROUGH ONE MAN…

Adam
Sin entered the world and we were all caught up in it' swirl.
Born into sin, as a slave, forgetting the gift God gave.
Death became the price, the payment due, our lives.
God sent commandment law; all people watched in awe
Breaking law-death reigned, nothing have we gained
In trespass many died, never being justified
Judgement came to pass, condemnation that will last
Everyone who disobeyed, A drastic price was paid
Trespass multiplied; more sinners truly died.
Hopeless in ours sins, nobody ever wins.

Christ
Christ, one human man, is the only one who can
Blameless, never sinned, He controls the wind
Sins forgiven, grace, is written on His face
Law will be no more, if we open the door
Life reigns, through His gift, Justification is swift
Righteousness, eternal life, Obedience ends the strife
All can choose the gift, He will our spirits lift
Forgiveness multiplied, not on the day He died
But on the day that He rose, if grace is what you chose!
Do you need help to cope, then just accept this hope!

SUN SWEPT

The sun swept over the dry barren land.
We labor and toil under its burning rays.
It is blistering our skin in vast, inescapable heat.
Mouths parched and lips cracking with thirst.

The sun swept over us day by day.
We try so hard to make some progress.
We hunger and thirst with no relief,
Just more of striving on the sun swept land.

The sun swept on, regardless of our pain.
The sun swept away all our hopes and dreams.
There is nothing more to wish for, only heat,
Frustration and futility are our constant companions.

The sun swept across the vast sky, for another day.
Another withers and perishes, still we go on.
How long can we endure? How much more can we take?
The unforgiving sun swept away everything of worth.

The suns swept up to its highest position,
And I hear a murmur from the tired and hopeless crowd.
In the distance, there is something new on the horizon.
No, it can't be, never anything new, just the sun sweeping by.

But wait, as all eyes turn to the eastern sky.
There is something new arising. What can it be?
Something sinister? Something to cause us more pain?
We see it rising and drawing nearer. How can it be?

The Son swept in on this glorious day.
He took care of all our hunger and thirst.

He healed our wounds and even our scars.
He brought back a glimmer of hope that was lost.

The Son swept in to save our souls,
And to heal our bodies, to free us.
Our bondage can be over in an instant
But sadly, any choose to stay bound.

How can they see and know and hear?
And experience, healing and filling and freedom,
Yet, choose to return to the routine of bondage,
As slaves to the sun swept, barren and harsh land?

If the Son sweeps by with freedom, healing and hope?
Will you choose to shake off the chains that bind you
In a desperate and barren land, without hope?

The choice is yours to make of your own free will.
Be swept away by hunger and thirst for sinful things
Or be swept away by the love of Christ into freedom?
My prayer is that you choose to be Son swept!

TURN, TURN, TURN

Turn in the springtime…

                In a fresh world dawning with hope
              Awaken with a quickening of your spirit.

Turn in the summer…

                In a hot, fiery passion for Christ
            Let others hearts be warmed by your heat.

Turn in the fall…

                As the leaves fall from the trees,
         Let your past sins fall from your remembrance.

Turn in the winter…

                Leave the chill outside and
            Curl up safe and warm in His arms.

Turn early in the morning…

                Rise with the sun
              Focusing on His glory.

Turn at night…

                He will help you to
              Sleep in restful peace.

Turn back in times of distance…

                He did not move away from you
              You moved away from Him.

Turn, Turn, Turn…

                Again, and again and again.

EN(COURAGE)

Courage is the ability to do something that is frightening to us,
or having strength in the face of pain.

Being brave, daring, audacious, fearless
Having grit, nerve, heroism and boldness.
On most days, this is not who we are, on our own
We often need someone else to urge us along.

Encourage is to fill another with courage, to sway
By giving our own support, confidence or hope away
We can cheer, coax, uplift, support and advise
Our words can reinvigorate and revitalize

Encourage others that you meet
Strengthen and inspire everyone you greet
Champion and persuade them with your support
All people, all kinds and every sort.

This is what we are all called to do
I accept the challenge, how about you?

ME VERSUS YOU

me, caught in stupidity and selfishness
      You send sensible people to bless

me, opinion and mouth are loud
      You want me wise, not proud

me, full of shame and disgrace
      You free me fully with Your grace

me, speaking words that destroy
      You send wisdom that brings joy

me, judging the guilty in pride
      You for these You love…You died

me, endless days of foolish talk
      You lift me up and help me walk

me, falling into the gossip trap
      You comfort hurt ones in Your lap

me, so very full of lazy days
      You want to teach me all Your ways

me, small, insignificant, lacking power
      You strong, Almighty, a safe tower

me seek security in things and money
      You forgive me with words, sweet as honey

me want to speak before I hear
      You always offer a ready ear

me in a battle, full of stress
>   You patiently waiting to bless

me broken and humble at last
>   You completely forgiving, all my past

me learning to stand, learning to trust
>   You knew Your plan was always just

me sought Your will and sought Your ways
>   You patiently waiting, Ancient of Days

me, "I need You Father from above"
>   You instantly came bearing Your love

me, "Come, Lord Jesus!"
>   You come to free us!

RESONATES

It resonates throughout all creation
It resonates in the vastness of the sky
It resonates in the depth of the sea
It resonates through the whole, entire earth

It resonates in my own mind, thoughts reaching to grasp it.
It resonates in my heart, emotions reaching to love it.
It resonates in my soul, searching and seeking to know it.
It resonates in eternity; past, present and future.

What is this that resonates all above, around and through us
Pulling and drawing us into quiet places to reflect
On its glory and purpose and meaning and sovereignty?
A song that reverberates deep in our souls from our first breath.

Oh, I have found it, I can know it and be certain of it
It fills me with joy, it is overwhelming in its intensity
It brings peace to my storms, security to my fears
love incomparable to my heart and light to my life

You ask, "What is it? Can I have it, too?"
Oh yes, you can, it is the exact same gift for you.
It is the call of mercy, grace and peace from above
Resonating through the creation He made in His love

Have you felt His call in the depths of your soul?
This creation displays His praise, to be seen by all.
He is ever calling and He is what and who resonates in everyone
Fall into this love, through faith in Jesus Christ, The Son

SINGULAR

Definition:
1. A word or form denoting or referring to just one person or thing.

2. Exceptionally good or great; remarkable, extraordinary, outstanding, notable, noteworthy, rare, unique, unparalleled, unprecedented, amazing, astonishing, phenomenal, astounding, fantastic, terrific.

There at the beginning of time with His Father, was the Word
To think He created all things, to some seems absurd
With His Father, truly Singular in every possible way
Every created thing, He gave life and light, on that day

He is the One True Light, coming into this world
All people so lost in darkness, as sinfulness swirled
The One and Only, took on flesh, blood and bone
Some saw His True Glory and no longer struggled alone.

He was the Singular Son of His Father, sent from above
Down to us, He bore all kindness, truth and love
He is the closest one to His Father, truly reflected for us
The Singular One taught, worked miracles and caused quite a fuss

The ones who get His Message, will with Him live forever
Back to the original plan of suffering alone and dying, never
This Singular Son could rightly bear condemnation
But His and His Father's love sent instead, salvation

There is a Singular Way, Truth and Life
It guides us through our struggle and our strife
If we want to meet His Father, there is only one way
Ask and I will show you and please do not delay

Just one person is all of these things: Exceptionally good, great, remarkable, extraordinary, outstanding, noteworthy, rare, unique, notable, unparalleled, unprecedented, amazing, astonishing, phenomenal, astounding, fantastic, terrific. and forgiving.

Also, He is the Singular, sinless Son of God who made atoning sacrifice for us
If you have not yet guessed, His name is Lord Jesus!

THE SON SHINE EFFECT

At the break of day, as I stood atop a hill, the sun began to rise.
A dark little cloud caught my attention.
It was the smallest and most insignificant cloud in the sky, just as black as it could be.
As the sun inched its way up the sky at daybreak, the dark little cloud began to change.
It turned dark blue and stayed that way for a while.
As the sun drew nearer to the dark little cloud it changed again to purple.
Every time the sun came closer to the cloud it changed again and again.
The cloud turned orange,
Then pink,
Then yellow
And finally, it became the most brilliant white that I had ever seen.
Just glancing at it made me want to shout and dance for joy.
This was God's gift to me!
Seeing that insignificant, little cloud transformed
Was a visual symbol of what He is doing in me.
I started out as a dark, little cloud.
And I stayed that way for a while.
But then, Jesus came and I began to change.
Moment by moment,
Glory to glory
As I draw nearer to Him-
I am changing!
I call this the Son shine effect.
And as I continue to walk with Him,
I know for certain that eventually
I will turn into that brilliant, white cloud,
That makes others want to shout and dance
Because they recognize that I have been with Him
And I have been transformed by His presence!

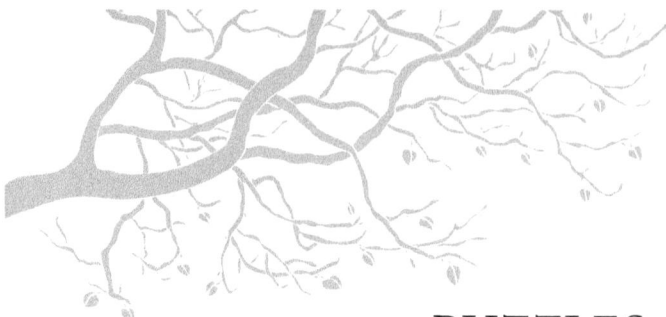

PUZZLES

As we make our way through life, we each begin to ponder our fate.

We are working puzzles in our minds, in an attempt to grasp the whole big picture.

Sometimes, the puzzle pieces flow together-as if guided by a Divine Hand.

At other times, we struggle and strive to make the pieces fit.

Occasionally, the pieces fall off the table to the floor and we are unaware. We continue working the puzzles and can't figure out what is missing. When we realize that something is missing, we go on a search to find the missing piece.

In some seasons, we are working our puzzles with tears running down our faces and falling onto it. Amazingly the Designer catches those tears and bottles them up, before they even land on a single piece to cause any damage.

At other times, we are distracted by the ease that someone else seems to have in putting their puzzle together or the amazing beauty of their picture and we get discouraged and turn away from our own puzzle for a while.

Still other times, we try putting the pieces of another person's puzzle into our own. This never works because the Designer did not design it that way and we must follow His plan.

Still, we go back to our own unique, individual puzzle and use all our resources of intelligence, emotion, agility, physical ability and conscience to guide us in completing our puzzle.

However, all of these resources are finite and will never achieve the goal of completing the puzzle, without the Master Plan of the One and Only Designer.

When we submit to following THE INSTRUCTION MANUAL, we begin to see more and more of the Designer's picture and it is breathtakingly beautiful.

Each piece added takes us closer and closer to that fate we are seeking, and it will be completed and achieved when we reach our Final Destination and the view at the end is more than we could ever have imagined!

The completed puzzle brings us peace, joy, and inspires awe for the Ultimate Designer, Who knew from the beginning what our end result would be!

SINISTER

Does it ever feel like the world is sinister against you? Even those you love seem to be against you. The truth is that this is an ultimate tool of the true sinister one, used to cause us pain, by giving us thoughts that the whole world is against us and out to get us. So many times, people who love us are hard on us because they see a potential in us that we don't see in ourselves or we don't believe we could ever possibly reach. They are trying to lead us in truth, but in our rebellious hearts they become enemies and we reject their truth, because we no longer trust them. We no longer believe they know or want what is best for us. Or we are trying so hard to please them and never seem to hit the mark and get their full approval. Always remember people who love you will discipline you to help you grow, never to hurt you.

The battle is in our own minds and hearts, not really having much to do with anyone else.

Answering the questions will lead you to the root of the problem:

1. According to God is the world good or evil?
2. Did God place those loved ones in your life for His purposes?
3. According to the Bible who is sinister against you, trying to trip you at every turn?
4. Do we have to believe every thought that comes into our mind?
5. What tools did God provide to fight these thoughts?
6. Can you win in the battlefield of your mind?
7. Does God provide discipline to those He loves?

Biblical answers:

1. Genesis 1:31a And God saw everything that he had made, and behold, it was very good.

2. Psalm 103:13 As a father shows compassion to his children, so the LORD shows compassion to those who fear him.

3. 1 Peter 5:8 Be sober-minded; be watchful. Your adversary the devil prowls around like a roaring lion seeking someone to devour. Resist him, firm in your faith, knowing that the same kinds of suffering are being experienced by your brotherhood throughout the world.

4. Isaiah 55:7-9 let the wicked forsake his way, and the unrighteous man his thoughts; let him return to the Lord, that he may have compassion on him, and to our God, for he will abundantly pardon. For My thoughts are not your thoughts, neither are your ways My ways, declares the Lord. For as the heavens are higher than the earth, so are My ways higher than your ways and My thoughts than your thoughts.

5. Ephesians 6:13-18 Therefore take up the whole armor of God, that you may be able to withstand in the evil day, and having done all, to stand firm. Stand therefore, having fastened on the belt of truth, and having put on the breastplate of righteousness, and, as shoes for your feet, having put on the readiness given by the gospel of peace. In all circumstances take up the shield of faith, with which you can extinguish all the flaming darts of the evil one; and take the helmet of salvation, and the sword of the Spirit, which is the word of God, praying at all times in the Spirit, with all prayer and supplication.

6. James 1:5 If any of you lacks wisdom, let him ask God, who gives generously to all without reproach, and it will be given him.

7. Psalm 94:12-15 Blessed is the man whom you discipline, O LORD, and whom you teach out of your law, to give him rest from the days of trouble, until a pit is dug for the wicked. For the LORD will not forsake his people; he will not abandon his heritage; for justice will return to the righteous, and all the upright in heart will follow it.

The choice is yours my friend. Accept correction as a loving act, not as a personal attack. Know that you can win the battlefield of the mind. Pray for those who hurt you, it is hard to be bitter with someone you are praying for.

Let your worth be determined by God, not people. Know for certain that you are enough, that God and your family truly love you and want the best for you. Turn to fight the real enemy Satan, WHO TRULY IS SINISTER AGAINST YOU, and would like to see nothing more than you walking around hurt, bitter and angry all the time. Do not let him win!

QUIET THE NOISE OF THE ENEMY!!!

Psalm 55:2-3

Attend to me, and answer me, I am restless in my complaint and I moan, because of the noise of the enemy, because of the oppression of the wicked. For they drop trouble upon me and in anger bear a grudge against me.

Noise is defined as any sound that is unwanted or interferes with one's hearing of something or someone.

Restless here is indicating an outward display of an inner attitude.

Enemy here is the plural form of the word. Anything and anyone that adds noise in our thoughts that distract us from seeking God (and the favorite tool of the Devil to keep us distracted).

NOISE NOISE NOISE NOISE noise ... peace

Across our lives we battle the noise that disturbs our soul's rest
Sneaking in as friends, family, social media, tv-whichever works best!

The enemy will get a grip on something that we dwell on
Anything or everything, but God has been his goal, all along!

When we gain peace about something and feel freedom there
He has already been laying a foundation to stop our prayer.

This can make us feel anxiety, dread and without hope
Remember, God has already given us what we need to cope.

The devil wants to block out the whisper that calls us to peace
Desires our acting out in sin and absolute, total defeat.

Over time, when we press on and continue chasing God's truth
The Lord can return us to innocence, as a child, in our youth.

Children have no worries, peace, energy and joy in abundance
This is His desire for the millions, the thousands, the hundreds.

I spent so many years letting the noise in my mind take over
Trying to hide, being closed off, ignoring my Soul and Spirit Lover.

But now, I have had so much experience battling the noise
I can see it, feel it and expect it before it arrives…meeting it with grace and poise.

Sin in this fallen world gives us a hard road to travel, with pain and strife
We only have to remember to look up to God, trust and rise.

When we do, we gain, with ease….

PEACE PEACE **PEACE PEACE PEACE**

AND ISN'T THAT WHAT WE WANTED ALL ALONG!

LOVE ON THE BATTLEFIELD

As a parent, when our kids are young...we fight for them.
Against anything that threatens, scares or may hurt them in any way.

As they grow, sometimes we find that we must fight with them.
When they are challenging their boundaries, or are outright rebellious.

The reasons and the goal in each situation are love, security, safety.
Our love for them will not allow us to give up or walk away...no matter what.

When they are threatened by any outside force each parent is willing to fight
with every weapon that they have available.

When the child is making choices that will harm their own peace or safety,
that parent steps right into the fray to challenge them on it.

Good parents stay the course, fight the good fight, never give up.
We know that the stakes are too high to do anything else.

Sometimes parenting is hard and painful to get through.
The hurt inflicted by your child is the hardest kind to bear.

We need to flip this script and remember that God is our Heavenly Father.
He fights for us and with us in every moment of our lives.

I can look back and see the hand of my Heavenly Father fighting for me as a child
And even now when I get myself in childish situations.

He is my Comforter when anything scares me or threatens me...
When I am under attack or may be hurt in some way.

We have all seen seasons of rebellion…when we tried to walk away
From God's security…thinking we could do it better on our own.

God loves each of us too much to stop pursuing us, in spite of ourselves.
His love for us will not allow Him to give up or walk away…no matter what.

He fights those outside forces that threaten us before we even realize we need help.
And His arsenal of weapons is all we could ever need.

When we make choices that will harm our own peace or safety…
The Good Shepherd is there to help us see the boundary line and bring us back into the fold.

God, the ultimate wise parent stays the course, fights the good fight, never gives up on us.
He knows that the stakes are too high to do anything else.

Sometimes we cause this Heavenly parent hardship and pain.
The hurt inflicted by His child is the hardest kind to bear…

And yet, He loves, He fights for and with us, He cries over us, He reaches out to us,
He pursues us and then…He welcomes the prodigal back home with open arms.

Psalm 136:1-9

O give thanks unto the Lord; for he is good:

                                    for his mercy endures forever.

O give thanks unto the God of gods:

                                    for his mercy endures forever.

O give thanks to the Lord of lords:

                                    for his mercy endures forever.

To him who alone does great wonders:

                                    for his mercy endures forever.

To him that by wisdom made the heavens:

                        for his mercy endures forever.

To him that stretched out the earth above the waters:

                        for his mercy endures forever.

To him that made great lights:

                        for his mercy endures forever:

The sun to rule by day:

                        for his mercy endures forever:

The moon and stars to rule by night:

                        for his mercy endures forever.

ABOUT THE AUTHOR

Renee Bennett is a follower of Christ, a wife, mother, grandmother, teacher and ministry leader. She leads women's mentoring for ladies in her community. She has traveled around the world on missions, with a focus on teaching the Bible to children of many cultures and reaching all people with the Gospel. Through one of these international connections, Renee is on the board of Enterprise Church Planting International (ECPI), which is based in Guyana, South America. ECPI is training up leaders who will travel all over the world to share the Gospel through relational teaching. Many decades of Bible study and journaling have led to inspiration for her to become an author who shares her knowledge with others to offer them hope. Her greatest wish is that others would be inspired to find their own word to research in the Bible and get to know more about God and his plan for them personally.

www.ingramcontent.com/pod-product-compliance
Lightning Source LLC
Chambersburg PA
CBHW071456070526
44578CB00001B/355